Isaiah

by Lynne M. Deming

General Editor, Lynne M. Deming
Assistant Editor, Margaret Rogers
Copy Processing, Sylvia Marlow
Cover Design by Harriet Bateman

ISBN 0-939697-20-3

Table of Contents

Outline of Isaiah

I. Prophecies from the Assyrian Domination (1:1–39:8)
   A. Isaiah's Memoirs (1:1–12:6)
      1. Oracles against Judah (1:1–5:30)
      2. The call of Isaiah (6:1-13)
      3. The Syro-Ephraimitic war (7:1–8:22)
      4. The messianic king (9:1-7)
      5. Judgment on Ephraim (9:8-21)
      6. No justice among the people (10:1-4)
      7. Judgment on Assyria (10:5-19)
      8. Remnant of Israel (10:20-23)
      9. Oracle of promise (10:24-27)
     10. The Assyrian threat (10:28-34)
     11. Oracles concerning the messiah (11:1-16)
     12. Concluding songs (12:1-6)
        a. A song of deliverance (12:1-3)
        b. A song of thanksgiving (12:4-6)
   B. Oracles Against Judah and Other Nations
     (13:1–23:18)
      1. Oracle against Babylon (13:1-22)
      2. Oracle against Babylon's king (14:1-23)
      3. Oracle against Assyria (14:24-27)
      4. Oracle against Philistia (14:28-32)
      5. Oracle against Moab (15:1–16:14)
      6. Oracle against Damascus (17:1-6)
      7. Oracle against idolatry (17:7-14)
      8. Oracles concerning Egypt (18:1–20:6)
      9. Oracle against Babylon (21:1-10)
     10. Oracle against Edom (21:11-12)
     11. Oracle against Arabia (21:13-17)
     12. Warning to Jerusalem (22:1-14)

Introduction to Isaiah 1–39

The prophet Isaiah was the son of Amoz, as the first verse in the book tells us. We know little or nothing about Isaiah's personal life. From reading Isaiah 6:1-8, some conclude that Isaiah was a priest in the Temple before he was called to prophesy. Isaiah's name means *Yahweh gives salvation.*

Chapters 1–39 are a collection of prophecies from the ministry of Isaiah the prophet. The later chapters in the book came from a later period, and were probably spoken and recorded by disciples of Isaiah the prophet.

Isaiah was a prophet of the Southern Kingdom (Judah). He directed his message to Judah, and especially Jerusalem, between 742 and 687 B.C. During this time, the Southern Kingdom was under the domination of Assyria, to the northeast. The Northern Kingdom (Israel) had ceased to exist as an independent nation about 722 B.C., when it fell to the Assyrians.

The first 39 chapters of Isaiah are divided into six main parts: the prophet's memoirs (Chapters 1–12), oracles concerning Judah and its neighbors (Chapters 13–23), the Isaiah Apocalypse (Chapters 24–27), oracles concerning Egypt (Chapters 28–32), post-exilic oracles (Chapters 33–36), and a historical appendix (Chapters 36–39).

Throughout these chapters Isaiah preaches a message of social justice, faith in God, rewards for the obedient, and judgment on the unfaithful. With this message Isaiah stands in the tradition of his contemporaries (Hosea, Micah, and Amos).

Isaiah 1–2

Introduction to These Chapters

Isaiah 1 contains a group of oracles that serve to introduce the rest of the book. Most of the elements found throughout Isaiah's prophecies are alluded to in this first chapter. Isaiah 2 begins with a short section describing the coming age (verses 2-5), and continues with a longer oracle on the day of the Lord.

Here is an outline of Isaiah 1 and 2.

I. Introductory Oracles (1:1-31)
   A. Superscription (1:1)
   B. Oracle to rebellious sons (1:2-3)
   C. Oracle to a sinful nation (1:4-9)
   D. Concerning religious practices (1:10-20)
   E. The fate of Jerusalem (1:21-28)
   F. Judah's faithlessness (1:29-31)
II. Oracles Concerning the Day of the Lord (2:1-22)
   A. Second superscription (2:1)
   B. The coming age (2:2-5)
   C. The day of the Lord (2:6-22)
      1. Judgment on idolatry (2:6-11)
      2. Judah's punishment (2:12-17)
      3. Judgment on idolatry (2:18-22)

Superscription (1:1)

The first verse in the Book of Isaiah sounds similar to the opening verses in many of the other Old Testament prophetic books. That is because this kind of introduction, called a *superscription*, is a basic form of prophetic speech. Not all superscriptions are worded in exactly the same way. But their purpose is always the same. They give us basic information we need to know about the prophet and his ministry. This superscription to Isaiah tells us the *who* (son of Amoz), the *what* (vision), the *where* (Judah), and the *when* (in the days of Uzziah, Jotham, Ahaz, and Hezekiah) of the prophet Isaiah.

As the introduction states, these kings reigned successively in Judah between the years 742 and 687 B.C. During this time, several significant events took place in Israel's history.

(1) Israel and Syria joined forces against the Assyrians (734 B.C.) but were unable to stand against the power of the Assyrian attack. They tried to persuade Judah to join forces with them, but Ahaz, king of Judah, allied with the Assyrians instead.

(2) Israel (the Northern Kingdom) fell to the Assyrians in 722/721 B.C.

(3) The Assyrians invaded the Philistine plain in 701 B.C. and devastated the city of Lachish.

(4) The reign of Hezekiah (726–687 B.C.) was dominated by a continual Assyrian threat.

Oracle to Rebellious Sons (1:2-3)

This short section is an exhortation directed to the *rebellious sons*, the children of Israel. The opening words get the attention of the audience. Oracles addressed to heaven and earth (in other words, everyone, everywhere) are common throughout the prophetic literature. By saying that the Lord has spoken, the prophet is assuring his audience that he speaks on God's behalf and with God's authority.

The second half of verse 2 begins a metaphor in which God, the father, chastises the people of Israel, his sons, for rebelling against him. According to the prophet, even lowly beasts understand what their response must be to their owner better than Israel understands its response to

God. Verse 3 uses the word *know* in the traditional Hebrew sense, which is different from our usual meaning of know (to be acquainted with). In the Hebrew language, to know means to be intimately associated with someone, in this case God. Isaiah is saying that the people of Israel are not in a right relationship to God. They have been rebellious by not putting their trust in God.

Oracle to a Sinful Nation (1:4-9)

The word *Ah*, which begins this section, is sometimes translated as *woe*. This word is commonly used in prophetic speech to indicate the beginning of a woe oracle. This woe oracle can be divided into two parts: verses 4-6 and verses 7-9.

The first two phrases in verse 4 are parallel; they could be translated *nation of sinners* and *people of iniquity*. A nation of sinners is a nation inhabited by people who have fallen short of God's expectations. The second two phrases are also parallel: *offspring of those who do evil,* and *sons of those who act corruptly*. The second half of verse 4 explains the nature of the people's sin. They have turned their backs on God. This judgment echoes the prophet's words in verse 2, above.

Verses 5 and 6 compare what has happened to the people of Israel to what happens to a rebellious slave at the hands of his master. The more the master beats the slave, the more the slave is disobedient. So it is with Israel. The more Israel is punished (symbolized by constant invasions by the enemies, especially Assyria), the more Israel continues to rebel. The prophet does not understand why Israel cannot change its ways.

Verses 7-9 focus on the devastation of the land. *Alien* refers to Israel's enemies. *The daughters of Zion* (verse 8) refers to the city of Jerusalem. Jerusalem has been plundered by enemies to the extent that it is now open and vulnerable, like a booth without walls. According to verse 9, however, the destruction has not been complete.

God has left a few survivors. Otherwise, Jerusalem would have met the same fate as Sodom and Gomorrah: total destruction by fire and brimstone (see Genesis 19).

Concerning Religious Practices (1:10-20)

This section is similar in its message to Amos 5:21-24 and Micah 6:6-8. God, through the prophet, is condemning certain of Israel's religious practices, especially those involving sacrifices. This section has two parts: words about sacrifice (verses 10-17), and a call for decision (verses 18-20).

Verse 10 introduces the words of God, which are spoken in verses 11-17. This oracle is addressed to the rulers of Sodom and the people of Gomorrah—in other words, the leaders and the common people. Everyone needs to hear this message. The prophet imagines that these persons are standing in the court of the Temple (verse 12), in the presence of God.

The speech in verses 11-17 begins with a rhetorical question, to which "nothing" is the expected answer. God is not like human beings. God does not need meat in order to survive. Verse 11 mentions sacrifices and burnt offerings, the two basic elements of Israel's sacrificial system. (See Leviticus 3 for a full description of these aspects of sacrifice.) Because the people have trampled God's courts when they appeared there (verse 12), God forbids any more offerings to be brought to the Temple. Verse 13 explains God's reason. God cannot tolerate iniquity and religious observance in the same setting.

Verses 16 and 17 focus on what is right about the worship of God. Right worship must involve purity of hands and heart alike. At the end of verse 17, the instructions are specific. To obtain God's favor one must care for the fatherless and the widow.

Verses 18-20 call for a decision on the part of the people. God and the people are opponents in an argument. In order to achieve purity of hands and heart,

the people must be obedient to God. Fulfilling ritual
obligations will not help. They must be obedient.

The Fate of Jerusalem (1:21-28)

This section opens with an accusation that the city of
Jerusalem, once faithful, has become a harlot. Justice and
righteousness used to characterize the people living there;
now they are murderers. *Your silver has become dross*
means that silver has turned into a waste product. What
was splendid in the past has turned out to be tarnished
and worthless. The people do not care for widows and
orphans, so they are not obedient (see 1:17).

The Mighty One of Israel (verse 24) refers to God. God's
will is for the purification of Jerusalem. To that end God
will punish the enemies of Judah, will remove the dross,
or waste products (lye helps to insure that all the dross is
removed), and will restore Jerusalem's leaders. After
these things are done, the city will become faithful as it
once was (verse 21). Verse 27 reinforces the idea that total
destruction is not in store for Jerusalem.

Judah's Faithlessness (1:29-31)

Forsaking the LORD and delighting in oaks refers to pagan
rituals of idol worship. Those who worship idols will
wither along with trees from which the idols are made.

Second Superscription (2:1)

This verse sounds quite similar to Isaiah 1:1. Possibly
this superscription is meant to introduce only the oracles
in Chapters 2–4, whereas 1:1 introduces the entire book.
Here, instead of a vision, Isaiah sees a *word* concerning
Judah and Jerusalem. Word means a message from God,
which Isaiah is charged to convey to his audience.

The Coming Age (2:2-5)

This oracle is repeated in Micah 4:1-4, with variations. It is
unclear whether the same prophecy was given

independently to these two prophets, or whether one prophet borrowed it from the other. Most scholars conclude that Isaiah borrowed it from Micah. Both prophets were active during the same time in Israel's history.

What will the coming age be like, according to this oracle? Zion (Jerusalem) will be lifted up higher than any surrounding mountains. Many people will come to Jerusalem to hear the law discussed and explained. Peace will reign, since weapons of war will be turned into implements of harvest. Verse 5 is addressed to the people directly. *The house of Jacob* is a reminder that they are descendants of Jacob, the father of Israel's twelve tribes.

Judgment on Idolatry (2:6-11)

Verse 2 is addressed to God, who has rejected the people because they condone the practices of divination and soothsaying, borrowed from their neighbors. The words *of diviners* are missing from the original Hebrew text. The Revised Standard Version (and other translations) inserts them on the basis of the parallel phrase of the soothsayers. Such practices were clearly forbidden by Israelite law (see Exodus 22:18, for example).

Verse 7 testifies to the current prosperity of Judah, which is also described in 2 Kings 15:1-7.

Verse 11 ends with the same formula that is found at the end of the next section (see 2:17). *In that day* refers to the day of the Lord, a theme found throughout the prophetic literature. At that time, God plans to intervene, bringing terror into the hearts of everyone present (verse 10).

Judah's Punishment (2:12-17)

It is mainly Judah's pride that will cause God's harsh judgment on that day in the future. Judgment is symbolized by a storm that will fell trees, tear down mountains, crush towns, tear down city walls, and dash ships to pieces. Tarshish is a distant city known for its ships carrying fine cargo.

Judgment on Idolatry (2:18-22)

This section describes the fate of the idols and those who worship them. The idols will utterly pass away. They will be abandoned by their worshipers when they begin crawling into caves to hide from the majesty of God. This section concludes with a warning to the effect that not only is it unwise to trust in idols, it is also foolish to trust in the human beings who make them. Trust should be given solely and completely to God.

§ § § § § § §

The Message of Isaiah 1–2

What do these introductory chapters to Isaiah's message tell us about what God is like?

§ God is a God who speaks through specific persons (Isaiah the prophet) to specific circumstances (what was happening in Judah in Isaiah's time).

§ God can be disappointed in and angry at the behavior of the people of Judah.

§ God can show displeasure at disobedience and rebellion. The consequences can be severe.

§ God will not bring about utter destruction. At least a few survivors will remain.

§ God is not pleased with ritual obligations performed in a context of disobedience or without justice.

§ Obedience will bring about rewards. Rebellion will bring about punishment.

§ The making of and worship of idols is a fruitless enterprise in God's eyes.

§ God's ultimate goal is the restoration of Jerusalem as the faithful city—a reign of peace.

§ § § § § § §

Isaiah 3–5

Introduction to These Chapters

Isaiah 3–5 contains oracles concerning Judah and Jerusalem, an allegory about a vineyard, and a series of woe oracles. These chapters can be outlined as follows.

The Collapse of the City (3:1-11)

These verses warn that God will punish Jerusalem by taking away *stay and staff*, that is, everything necessary for life to be sustained. These necessary items include food, water, and the city's leaders. Verses 2 and 3 list the persons necessary for the ongoing existence of the city: mighty men, soldiers, judges, prophets, diviners, elders, captains, counselors, magicians, and experts in charms. Verses 4 and 5 indicate that when Jerusalem is stripped of its leaders, anarchy will reign. Ironically, the young and naive will *rule* in the places of the experienced, producing unrest and eventually violence (verse 4).

Verses 8 and 9 give the reason for Jerusalem's collapse: the sins of the people. They have rebelled against God. The prophet is making a close connection between a crisis in the political structure of the city and a crisis in the relationship between God and the people.

Verses 10 and 11 come from the wisdom tradition. They make the point that all persons are responsible for their own fates (they have brought evil upon themselves).

God and Jerusalem's Leaders (3:12-15)

In verse 12, God addresses the people in the first person, uttering a lament over them. They are in such an unfortunate state that they are ruled by women and children. Also, their leaders mislead them. Thus God is judging both the people who allow themselves to be misled, and the leaders who mislead them.

The judgment is given in verses 14-15, introduced in verse 13. The elders and princes (leaders of the people) are to be judged on account of their taking advantage of the people and of their power and authority over them. The people were entrusted to their leaders just as a vineyard is entrusted to its owner, and the leaders took advantage of the situation. That God is angry is shown by the tone of the question in verse 15.

The Women of Jerusalem (3:16–4:1)

Verse 16 introduces this section by stating the problem: The women of Jerusalem are wanton and ostentatious. They are too concerned with the way they look. Verse 17 describes God's judgment. Verses 18-24 elaborate on what will be taken from them.

Verse 25 is a direct address to a woman (the word *your* is singular in the Hebrew). This woman represents the city of Jerusalem. Verse 25 and 4:1 continue the thought, but in the third person. This short section describes a situation resulting from military defeat. The women of the city have lost their husbands in battle, and so have lost their protection. Their situation makes them desperate enough to humiliate themselves.

Restoration of Jerusalem (4:2-6)

The *branch* of the Lord refers to the remnant that will be left in Jerusalem after the destruction. The fruit, or produce, or outcome, will be a return to the restored city. *Everyone who has been recorded* alludes to a book in which names of the righteous were written. (See Revelation 20:12, 15; Daniel 12:1.)

The cloud, smoke, and fire are symbols of the presence of God. These elements were present as God and the people went out of Egypt and into the Promised Land, hundreds of years earlier. These verses form the end of a major section that began at 3:1. Note that God's last word on the subject of Jerusalem is not judgment, but hope.

Song of the Vineyard (5:1-7)

The song of the vineyard is one of the most beautiful poetic passages in the Old Testament. It is an allegory about a vineyard and its owner, and it teaches us about the relationship between God and the people of Israel.

The poem may have been composed in honor of a special occasion in Israel, perhaps a feast or some other kind of religious celebration. The prophet asks his audience to imagine themselves in the middle of a crowded street in Jerusalem. The singer gets the attention of those around him and then begins to sing the song. The first part of verse 1 introduces the song. Unfortunately, the audience is not told who the singer's friend is, and neither are we.

The owner of the vineyard took great pains to take care of it in the proper way. Because the vineyard was on a hill, it probably received plenty of sunlight, and we know that the soil was fertile. All these factors would seem to point toward a bountiful harvest. Indeed, this is what the owner expected, since he went to the trouble of building a watchtower in the middle of the vineyard (rather than a temporary structure to use just during the time of harvest). However, at the end of verse 2 we read of the owner's great disappointment. He asks himself, why are they so small and sour (wild)? Jeremiah 31:30 indicates what happens when one tries to eat wild grapes.

What went wrong? The singer asks the crowd this question in verses 3 and 4, just as the singer's friend (the owner of the vineyard) must have asked himself. In these verses, however, the song begins to shift in orientation. Now the owner of the vineyard begins to speak. The audience probably begins to realize at this point, as do we, that this song is more than just a story about a vineyard that didn't produce.

In traditional biblical imagery, the vineyard is a metaphor for the people of Israel, and the owner of the vineyard represents God. Matthew uses these same symbols in his parable of the wicked tenants. (See Matthew 21:33-44.) So in verse 4, the owner of the vineyard (God) is asking the people to judge what more he could have done for the vineyard (the people of Israel). The only possible answer was, "nothing more." In effect, the people of Judah are being asked to pass judgment on themselves. They are sour, wild grapes. They are a grave disappointment.

In verses 5-7 God reveals the punishment for the people's failure. The people, represented by the vineyard, will be removed, devoured, trampled on, and ignored. God will break down the wall around the vineyard, leaving it undefended, just as the people will be left undefended. Their enemies will trample them.

Just in case the audience missed the point of the allegory, verse 7 makes the comparison very clear. *The vineyard of the LORD of hosts* is the house of Israel. Just as the owner of the vineyard looked for juicy, red grapes, God looked for justice and righteousness from the people. Just as the vineyard owner was disappointed in the results of his effort, so God is disappointed in the response of the people. Justice and righteousness are important concepts in the prophetic tradition. (See Amos 5:24, for example.) *Justice* refers to the way persons behave, and *righteousness* refers to the relationship between persons and God.

Woe Oracles (5:8-23)

This section contains six woe oracles. The woe oracle is a common form of prophetic speech. (See Amos 5:18.)

First Woe (5:8-10)

Woe to those who join house to house is a warning against covetousness, or greed. Literally, the prophet is referring to the practice of buying up smaller properties whose owners are in financial trouble. The judgment on persons who accumulate property in this way is that their land will not produce. A ten-acre vineyard will produce only one bath (six gallons) of grapes. A homer (five bushels) of seeds will produce only an ephah (half a bushel) of grain.

Second Woe (5:11-17)

This woe passes judgment on those who consume too much alcohol. They spend too much time drinking and carousing, and not enough time cultivating their relationship with God. The prophet Amos also warns against this kind of lifestyle (see Amos 6:4-6).

This second woe oracle is followed by a section (verses 13-17) that describes the future punishment of Israel. Because of the sin of the people, and because the whole people will be punished, *Sheol* (the underworld) will have to expand its borders *(opened its mouth beyond measure)*. The prophet uses a graphic image of the underworld as a huge animal waiting to swallow people up. The leaders and people in Jerusalem go *down* and are swallowed in Sheol. In contrast to the sinful people, God is a God of justice and righteousness (verse 16).

Third Woe (5:18-19)

This woe is a warning to those who presume to taunt God. Just as surely as a cart is drawn when it is attached to oxen with ropes, those who mock God will bring punishment upon themselves. These persons say, in effect, "If God can do so much, let God prove it to us."

Fourth Woe (5:20)

This woe warns against unethical behavior. Persons who twist their situation to their own advantage will bring down God's wrath upon themselves.

Fifth Woe (5:21)

The fifth woe is uttered against those who have an exaggerated opinion of themselves. This verse is reminiscent of wisdom sayings found in the Book of Proverbs (see 26:12, for example).

Sixth Woe (5:22-23)

This woe is similar in its message to the second woe in 5:11-12. Those who drink too much alcohol and boast about it, or who brag about being able to mix strong drinks, will be judged. In like manner, officials who take bribes in order to judge others innocent, thereby subverting the legal system, will be punished for their behavior.

Judgment on Judah (5:24-30)

Because the people have rejected God's law, *their root will be as rottenness.* Without roots or blooms, the entire plant would surely disappear. The same will happen to people who have ignored the word and will of God.

In verse 25, the poem suddenly switches to the past tense. The message is that God has brought judgment in the past. God will do so again in the future. The outstretched arm of God is a common image in the historical traditions (see, for example, Exodus 32:11; Deuteronomy 6:15).

Verses 26-29 describe an attack on Judah by an enemy, probably the Assyrians (*a nation afar off*). This attack is the symbol of God's judgment for the sin of the people. The army is well organized and enthusiastic. Their weapons are the best, their horses are strong, their chariots are good, and they will be successful against Judah.

Verse 30 concludes the first five chapters of Isaiah with an allusion to the cosmic darkness expected at the end of time.

§ § § § § § §

The Message of Isaiah 3-5

§ God was active in Israel's early history, God was active in Isaiah's time, and God is active now. God has the power to summon the forces of heaven and earth.

§ Trouble and unrest in the political/social circumstances of Jerusalem are symptomatic of trouble in the relationship between God and the people.

§ Being in a right relationship with God means being in right relationships with other human beings and with ourselves.

§ God will insure that a remnant of survivors remains after destruction.

§ God can be disappointed in the response on the part of the people. Disappointment due to the sin of the people will bring punishment.

§ God uses other nations (such as Assyria) as a means of punishment.

§ § § § § § §

Isaiah 6

Introduction to This Chapter

Isaiah 6 contains the call of the prophet. Using vivid imagery and majestic language, the prophet narrates his experience in the Temple in Jerusalem, when God commissioned him to prophesy to the people of Judah.

Here is an outline of Isaiah 6.

I. The Vision of the Prophet (6:1-4)
II. The Prophet Is Commissioned (6:5-13)
  A. Initial response (6:5)
  B. The prophet is cleansed (6:6-8)
  C. The message is conveyed (6:9-13)

The Vision of the Prophet (6:1-4)

The first few words in verse 1 date the occurrence of Isaiah's call. The year that Uzziah, king of Judah, died was 742 B.C. Isaiah introduces the description of his vision with the words *I saw*. These words are commonly used to introduce visions in the prophetic literature. The phrase makes this and other visions "official," from God.

The prophetic literature contains many reports of many visions. But very rarely does a prophetic vision involve the image of God. The prophet Ezekiel also sees God enthroned, and gives more details of God's appearance than Isaiah does. (See Ezekiel 1:26-28.)

In Isaiah's vision, God is seated upon a *throne*, probably a reference to the ark of the covenant. The prophet's brief description of God is intended to convey majesty and power. God is *high and lifted up*. God's garment (train) is so large that it fills the whole Temple. God is larger than (human) life.

Verse 2 describes the seraphim that hover over God. They represent the linking of heaven and earth in the vision. These winged creatures, which were serpents of some kind, probably corresponded to the Uraei, serpents who protected God in Egyptian mythology. These seraphim had six wings apiece. Two of these wings covered the seraph's face, two of them covered his feet (a euphemism for genitals), and two were used for flying.

Verse 3 repeats the song of praise that one seraph sings to another. In the Hebrew language, repetition is one way to add emphasis to a statement or idea. This song of praise begins by repeating the word *holy* three times. By saying that God is *holy, holy, holy,* the song is praising God as holy to the infinite degree. The same kind of threefold repetition for emphasis is found in Jeremiah 7:4.

The Lord of hosts, *Yahweh Sebaoth* in Hebrew, is the cultic name for God that was used in temple worship. The name signifies God's power over heaven and earth.

The exact meaning and origin of the word *Sebaoth* (usually translated *of hosts*) is uncertain. The original reference may have been to the armies of Israel and/or Judah. In this case, the God of hosts would have been the God who led the Israelite and Judean armies in battle. Or perhaps the word is more abstract, and simply means all-powerful. The origin of the term, whether Canaanite (pre-Israelite) or Israelite, is also unclear.

The whole earth is full of his glory brings the power of God to an earthly level. God's glory means God's dignity and respect. In the priestly tradition, the glory of God was thought to be hidden behind the cloud (see Exodus 16:10). This same concept appears in the New Testament when the shepherds encounter the angels who tell them the good news of Jesus' birth (see Luke 2:9). The earth as full of God's glory is mentioned as a hope of the psalmist at the end of Psalm 72 (verse 19).

The song of praise sung by the seraph had a profound effect. It caused the foundations of the Temple to tremble. That powerful image is also part of the final vision in the Book of Amos (see Amos 9:1-4). In addition to the shaking of the foundations, the Temple was filled with smoke. The smoke shielded the eyes of the prophet from the image of God, which was important since no one can look at the face of God and live. (See Exodus 33:20.) Smoke and fire are often used as symbols to indicate the presence of God, called a *theophany*.

Initial Response (6:5)

In this verse the prophet speaks in the first person. His response seems somewhat surprising at first. Why would a vision of God cause the prophet to say *Woe is me*? Why did the prophet not respond joyfully to being in the presence of God? Since he is *a man of unclean lips*, the prophet cannot stand in the presence of God or join in the song of praise. We know from the cultic regulations in the Book of Leviticus that unclean things (and persons) are an abomination to God. (See Leviticus 11:24-45.) The prophet immediately becomes aware of his guilt and the guilt of his people, and he responds accordingly.

The Prophet Is Cleansed (6:6-8)

One of the seraphim takes a burning coal from the altar, using a pair of tongs. He touches the mouth of the prophet, his unclean lips, with the burning coal. This act of purification on the part of the seraph takes away the prophet's sin and guilt. Symbolically, the guilt of the whole people is taken away. After this purification, the prophet is free to respond and to be used for God's purposes.

Verse 8 gives the prophet's response. The questions God asks sound similar to the words used when Moses was commissioned to lead the people out of Egypt. (See Exodus 3:10.) The prophet assumes God's questions are directed to him.

Without hesitation, the prophet responds positively. *Here am I* is a common response to requests and commands made by God. Abraham had a similar response when God put him to the test (see Genesis 22:1). In most of the other prophetic call narratives, there is initial hesitation on the part of the prophet when he is confronted with the task. (See Exodus 4:10; Jeremiah 1:6.) This tradition of initial hesitation makes it all the more remarkable that Isaiah responds quickly and positively. His claim to be a man of unclean lips, sometimes said to indicate hesitation, is really an admission of guilt. Besides, it was uttered before the actual call was issued.

The Message Is Conveyed (6:9-13)

Now God tells the prophet what the essence of his message will be. The people are commanded to hear, and see, but for all their efforts they will be unsuccessful. *Hear and hear, but do not understand. See and see, but do not perceive.* These words are quoted by Jesus in the tenth chapter of Matthew. Note the way God instructs Isaiah to speak to *this people*. The tone sounds bitter and angry.

Verse 10 continues the message. The heart of the people will become fat, so that it will beat more sluggishly. Their ears and eyes will be closed. In various ways, then, the senses of the people will be dulled to the ways of God and the words of the prophet.

Why would God charge Isaiah to dull the senses of the people? A careful reading shows the words in these verses to describe the *effect* of the prophet's activity, not the content of the message he is to convey. God will punish the people through the vehicle of the prophet.

In verse 11 Isaiah raises the question, *How long O Lord?* This question is a formula used often in the laments of the Old Testament, especially in the psalms of lament (Psalm 13:1, for example). With this question, the prophet is not asking how long he will be prophesying this message to the people. Instead, he is asking how long the people's senses will be dulled. The answer comes immediately—until the message is received and responded to. But then it will be too late. Destruction will have already taken place.

Verse 12 refers to the future exile of Judah to Babylon, which occurred in 587 B.C.

Verse 13 sounds a note of hope. One-tenth of the population will survive the destruction. However, even that remnant will be *burned again*, like a tree stump that begins to grow new shoots which are then destroyed, but not totally. Just enough growth is left so that the stump can eventually grow into a new tree. The last part of verse 13 is awkward and difficult to translate.

Taken as a whole, Isaiah 6:1-13 functions as an introduction to the major section that follows, about the Syro-Ephraimitic War (through 9:6). As we read this section of Isaiah we are struck with the courage of this prophet. Far from hesitating to fulfill his calling, the prophet offers to be the messenger almost before he is asked. He is not afraid to be in God's presence. Nor is he afraid to proclaim God's message, difficult as it is to hear.

§ § § § § § §

The Message of Isaiah 6

§ God does not hesitate to use the prophet as a vehicle to proclaim the message. Nor does God hesitate to carry out the punishment that has been set.

§ Once purified (forgiven), a formerly sinful human being can now speak on God's behalf.

§ God leaves an element of hope with the prophet. Destruction will not be complete; a stump will remain as the beginning of a new tree.

§ § § § § § §

PART FOUR Isaiah 7–9

Introduction to These Chapters

Isaiah 7–9 is a series of oracles, most of which are related in some way to the Syro-Ephraimitic War. In 734–732 B.C., Syria, Judah, and Israel were involved in skirmishes connected to the advancing Assyrian threat. Pekah, king of Israel (the Northern Kingdom), and Rezin King of Syria (to the north) allied with each other in a effort to stand against the Assyrians. They tried to convince Ahaz, king of Judah (the Southern Kingdom), to join with them in their alliance. Eventually Rezin and Pekah besieged Jerusalem, but could not subdue the city. Ahaz, against the advice of Isaiah, chose to ally with Tiglath-Pileser, the Assyrian king. The Assyrians subsequently defeated both Syria and Israel.

Against this background we have Isaiah 7–9. Here is an outline of these chapters.

I. The Syro-Ephraimitic War (7:1–8:22)
  - A. The sign of Shear-Jashub (7:1-9)
  - B. The sign of Immanuel (7:10-17)
  - C. Further threats (7:18-25)
  - D. The sign of Maher-Shalal-hash-baz (8:1-4)
  - E. Miscellaneous Oracles (8:5-10)
  - F. Binding the testimony (8:11-22)

II. The Messianic King (9:1-7)

III. Judgment on Ephraim (9:8-21)
  - A. Pride brings punishment (9:8-12)
  - B. The leaders are corrupt (9:13-17)
  - C. Immorality among the people (9:18-21)

The Sign of Shear-Jashub (7:1-9)

Verses 1-9 of Chapter 7 describe an encounter between Isaiah and Ahaz, king of Judah. As the first few words of verse 1 indicate, Ahaz was the son of Jotham, and his successor on the Judean throne. As this narrative will indicate, the reputation of King Ahaz was not a positive one. (See also 2 Kings 16:1-4.)

Rezin, the king of Syria to the north, and Pekah, king of Israel, combined forces to wage war against Judah. But as verse 1 indicates, they were not successful. Note the similar wording between Isaiah 7:1 and 2 Kings 16:5. In fact, 2 Kings 16:1-20 is the historical narrative that parallels the prophetic account in Isaiah 7:1-9.

When the kingdom of Judah is threatened, the whole line of David is threatened. This narrative stresses that fact when the words *the house of David* are used rather than *King Ahaz* or *Judah*. That the royal line of David is in jeopardy heightens the tension of the situation and increases the importance of the events that are about to take place.

Ephraim is another name for Israel, the Northern Kingdom. Perhaps Ephraim is used instead of Israel because of the negative impression the reader gets of the actions of the Northern Kingdom.

The message that Ahaz receives, that *Syria is in league with Ephraim,* is potentially devastating. The Davidic monarchy is in danger. The house of David is God's chosen dynasty; it is under God's protection. The people are afraid, and so they *shake as the trees of the forest shake before the wind.*

Verses 3-9 report God's commissioning of Isaiah to convey a message to King Ahaz. God is very specific, telling the prophet exactly where he should go, whom he should meet, and whom he should take along with him. Isaiah's son's name, Shear-jashub, symbolizes hope for the future as well as the coming destruction. The name means *only a remnant will return.* In asking Isaiah to bring his son along, God indicates that the outcome of the encounter is already clear. Ahaz will not listen, and destruction will follow.

Verse 4 begins the actual message. God's admonition to Ahaz is that he should be absolutely fearless, and should take no action. In effect, God is saying to Ahaz, "It's not as bad as it looks." The command to be fearless and passive is reminiscent of the words in Isaiah 30:15: *In returning and rest you shall be saved; in quietness and in trust shall be your strength.* After all, these two kingdoms (Syria and Israel) were already going to be destroyed. Ahaz should have nothing to fear from them.

Syria and Israel are called *two smoldering stumps of firebrands.* The message is that the smoke they are creating is the kind of smoke that comes from dying embers in a fire.

Verse 5 indicates where the blame should be placed—who is really responsible. Syria has initiated the action and Israel has followed along. The same assumption is made in the historical account of the events found in 2 Kings 16 (see verses 5-9).

Verse 6 mentions the *son of Tabeel* as the person Rezin wanted to install on the throne of Judah as its puppet king. The identity of this person is unknown. Perhaps he was one of Judah's leaders who originally came from the region of Tabeel, located in the northern part of Syria-Palestine. Or perhaps he was the son of a man whose name was Tabeel.

In verses 7-9 the message continues. Damascus is the capital of Syria; Rezin is the ruler in Damascus. Within sixty-five years Ephraim (Israel) will be destroyed. We know that the Assyrians conquered Samaria, Israel's capital, in 722 B.C., sixty-five years earlier. In fact, this prophecy must be dated sometime after 742, at the time of Isaiah's call. Some scholars think a historical editor inserted notes such as these all through the book of Isaiah, after the prophecies were first written down.

The first part of verse 9 parallels the first part of verse 8. Samaria is the capital of Israel (Ephraim), and the son of Remaliah (Pekah) rules in Samaria.

The last part of verse 9 is a special warning to King Ahaz. Isaiah makes it clear to Ahaz that the survival of the house of David depends on what Ahaz decides. When David was king, some 200 years earlier, God promised him that his dynasty would endure forever. (See 2 Samuel 7:16.) Now that earlier promise is placed in jeopardy. Because of Ahaz's decision, the state of Judah eventually fell to the Babylonians in 587 B.C.

The Sign of Immanuel (7:10-17)

This famous passage has an especially important place in the history of the Christian tradition. The Gospel of Matthew quotes 7:14 as a prophecy fulfilled with the birth of Jesus (see Matthew 1:18-25).

Verse 10 begins with the word *again*, showing a continuity in the narrative with what has preceded. God tells Ahaz to ask for a sign, so that he might believe in the message God is sending him. God says, "I'll do anything, whether it is *as deep as Sheol or high as heaven.*" But Ahaz refuses to test God (verse 12).

When verse 13 begins the prophet himself is speaking, since he speaks of God in the third person. Isaiah's impatience with Ahaz shows through here. It is bad enough, according to Isaiah, that Ahaz is stubborn when it comes to dealing with other persons. But it is even worse to be stubborn in one's dealings with God! God will give you a sign anyway, whether you want it or not. Note that Isaiah calls God *my God*. This label indicates that the prophet realizes Ahaz has already made his decision. He now has no right to call God *my God*.

Behold, a young woman (virgin) shall conceive and bear a son, and shall call his name Immanuel (God is with us). The Hebrew word translated *young woman* means a girl of marriageable age. This same word is used in Genesis

24:43 to refer to Rebekah and in Exodus 2:8 to refer to Moses' sister. The Septuagint translates this word as *parthenos* (virgin), and Matthew 1:23 interprets the word in Isaiah 7:14 to mean a virgin. Clearly, the Matthean quote of Isaiah 7:14 assumes that this passage is a prophecy about the birth of Jesus. However, Matthew re-interprets 7:14 into a special set of circumstances.

By naming her son Immanuel, this woman shows her trust in God. Verse 14 describes what this child will be like and what will happen to him when he is old enough to distinguish between good and evil. What does it mean that Immanuel will eat cream and honey? In 7:22, cream and honey designate a time of plenty, for those who survived the devastation. Thus, cream and honey are the food for times of salvation. Before that time, however, there will be devastation to Syria and Israel (Ephraim). Verse 17 continues the threat, applying it to Judah as well.

Further Threats (7:18-15)

Verses 18-25 contain four threats that elaborate on the judgment announced in 7:17. The first threat (verses 18-19) describes the actual attack on Judah by the Assyrian forces. The second threat (verse 20) uses metaphorical language to describe the wiping away of Judah and its population at the hands of the Assyrians. The third threat (verses 21-22) is not really a threat, but a promise of messianic salvation, in which the survivors of the devastation will live a life of abundance. The fourth threat (verses 23-25) describes what will happen to the land itself. In a word, the land will be worthless.

The Sign of Maher-Shalal-hash-baz (8:1-4)

Once again we have a narrative related to the Syro-Ephraimitic War. Isaiah is commanded by God to take a large tablet and write upon it *Belonging to Maher-Shalal-hash-baz*. Two witnesses are summoned to attest to the fact that Isaiah carried out God's command.

The other half of Isaiah's symbolic action has to do with his second son. This time the mother is a prophetess. Isaiah is to name this son Maher-Shalal-hash-baz, which means *the spoil speeds, the prey hastes.* In other words, and as verse 4 explains, there still is a chance for Ahaz to turn the situation in Judah around. Syria and Israel are about to be *carried away before the King of Assyria.*

Miscellaneous Oracles (8:5-10)

The prophet continues with another message from God. The people have *refused the waters of Shiloah,* a stream running through the city of Jerusalem. This stream is contrasted to *the waters of the river* (Euphrates), which God will bring upon them like a mighty flood. The River here symbolizes Assyria, where it is located.

Verses 9-10 change the mood of this section. After the prophet has promised disaster for the people in verses 5-8, here he speaks to the *far countries,* enemies of Judah, to the effect that Judah is under God's protection. All their efforts *will come to nought,* in the end.

Binding the Testimony (8:11-22)

This section is the prophet's first-person narrative describing the binding and sealing of the testimony. It is introduced by verses 11-15, and is a kind of prophetic teaching on what God can do on behalf of the people. The narrative begins with a formula that is often used in the prophetic literature to introduce a message from God. *The Lord spoke thus to me . . . .* The main point made in verses 12-13, which contain several pieces of advice from God to the prophet, is that God is the one to be feared and revered, not one's earthly enemies.

Verses 14 and 15 prophesy that God will become a stumbling block to the two *houses of Israel* (Israel and Judah). There is irony in this statement, since the Old Testament many times refers to God as a rock of refuge and strength for the people to count on. (See Psalm 18:2, for example.) In this passage, God is described as a rock that will get in the way of the people's survival.

Verses 16-22 describe the binding and sealing of the testimony, or teaching. Binding the testimony preserves the content, and sealing it guarantees that it is authentic when it is discovered and used sometime in the future. In ancient times, documents that were bound and sealed were kept in earthenware jars. What the prophet means here by testimony, or teaching, is the content of the instructions that God has given him.

Verse 17 states that although God has turned aside from the people, the prophet will continue to hope for a bright future. Verses 19-20 are a polemic against the superstitious, and the practices of mediums, wizards, and sorcerers. When God turns away from the people, it would be natural for them to turn elsewhere for help. But Isaiah argues against this temptation. The people should wait for further word from the Lord, obeying what has been revealed thus far (verse 20).

The Messianic King (9:1-7)

Verse 1 of Chapter 9 indicates that the prophet is moving from judgment to promise in his message to his audience. In the original Hebrew text, this verse is the last verse in Chapter 8. In the Hebrew, Chapter 9 begins with the English verse 2. These verses sound much like the hymns of thanksgiving we find in the Psalter. (See Psalm 21, for example.)

Verse 1 mentions Zebulun and Naphtali. These areas are in the northern part of the country, which later came to be called Galilee. *The way of the sea* refers to the route between Damascus and the Mediterranean Sea. The Assyrians probably used this route in their march on Judah. Verse 2 describes the future deliverance of God's people in metaphorical language (*darkness and light*).

Verse 2 addresses God directly, offering praise for the joy the people are experiencing because of their future deliverance. In verses 4-7, the reasons for the people's joy are given. God has broken the yoke of oppression that lay on the people, God has broken the staff, and has broken the rod of their oppressor. *As on the day of Midian* refers to a battle in which Gideon fought against high odds and defeated a Midianite army (see Judges 7). God has also defeated the enemy (verse 5). And God has restored the house of David by sending a king (verses 6-7).

This king will have the authority of the government on his shoulder. He is given four names in this prophecy. *Wonderful counselor* refers to his integrity in the political sphere. *Mighty God* stresses his power. *Everlasting Father* signifies his care for the people. *Prince of Peace* shows his ability to bring lasting peace to the nation. Verse 7 summarizes the lasting effect this king will have.

Pride Brings Punishment (9:8-12)

These verses are addressed to the Northern Kingdom (Ephraim, or Israel), of which Samaria was the capital. The prophet describes in symbolic language the defeat of the land by its enemies. The Syrians dwell north of Israel, and the Philistines inhabit the area directly to the west along the Mediterranean seacoast.

The Leaders Are Corrupt (9:13-17)

This prophecy judges both the corrupt leaders who led the people astray, and the people who allowed themselves to be led. Note the use of *this people* in a derogatory tone (as in 6:10).

Immorality Among the People (9:18-21)

Moral corruption *burns like a fire* among the people. Ultimately, the people will bring destruction upon themselves. The people are greedy, stealing from their neighbors and never getting enough. The prophet is alluding to the fact that the neighbors Israel and Judah have turned against one another (see 7:1-9).

The Message of Isaiah 7–9

These chapters are some of the most important in all of the Old Testament prophetic literature. What message do they contain about God and God's relationship to the world?

§ The house of David is God's chosen house. God is willing to work through the prophet to bring about the downfall of the Davidic dynasty, for the ultimate goal of a restored community.

§ Sometimes God wants to be put to the test. When Ahaz would not cooperate, the downfall of the Southern Kingdom came one step closer.

§ If King Ahaz had trusted God rather than becoming involved in political manuevers with Assyria, he could have saved himself and his kingdom.

§ God, although resolved to punish the people for their disobedience, holds out hope for restoration. To think of a day when humankind will live an abundant life helps us to live through the dark times in our lives. That same hope helped Ahaz through times of despair.

§ God is the Lord of hosts, the mighty God. Isaiah used *Yahweh Sebaoth* (Lord of hosts) to remind his audience that God is all-powerful. The power of God is our assurance of ultimate restoration.

§ God knew that the people of Judah would not heed the warnings they were given. God sent Isaiah to harden their hearts rather than to change their minds. In that way, destruction would surely happen, causing the people to repent and change their ways.

§ § § § § § §

Introduction to These Chapters

Isaiah 10–12 are the final three chapters in the first portion of the book. They contain a collection of various kinds of prophetic oracles, including a messianic oracle, a woe oracle, and an oracle of promise.

Here is an outline of these chapters.

I. Miscellaneous Oracles (10:1-34)
   A. No justice among the people (10:1-4)
   B. Judgment on Assyria (10:5-19)
   C. Remnant of Israel (10:20-23)
   D. Oracle of promise (10:24-27)
   E. The Assyrian threat (10:28-34)
II. Oracles Concerning the Messiah (11:1-16)
   A. The messianic king (11:1-9)
   B. The messianic age (11:10-16)
III. Concluding Songs (12:1-16)
   A. A song of deliverance (12:1-3)
   B. A song of thanksgiving (12:4-6)

No Justice Among the People (10:1-4)

Verses 1-4 utter a warning to all those who corrupt justice. The theme of these verses is the same as that of the previous section, so it is likely that 10:1-4 concludes the longer oracle that began at 9:8.

Iniquitous decrees are those that ignore the rights of widows and orphans. The second part of verse 1 indicates that these decrees were put into writing. Verse 2 mentions the ones who suffer on account of these decrees—the needy, the poor, the widows, and the fatherless. We know that these persons had God's special care and concern (see Exodus 22:22-27, for example).

Verse 4 is a vivid image of the rich kneeling among the prisoners on account of the oppression they have caused.

Judgment on Assyria (10:5-19)

This long section conveys the message that Assyria will surely be destroyed on account of its pride. Although verse 5 would seem to indicate that the message is spoken directly to Assyria, it is really a condemnation of Assyria given through the prophet's audience, the people of Judah. (Assyria is spoken of in the third person in verse 6.) Assyria is God's instrument, used for both the punishment and the restoration of Judah.

This accusation against Assyria is twofold: He is greedy (verse 7), and his leaders are proud (verse 13).

Verse 9 mentions Calno, Carchemish, Hamath, Arpad, Samaria, and Damascus. Carchemish was located on the Euphrates River; it was originally a Hittite city. It was conquered by the Assyrians in the eighth century, as was Calno (located south of Carchemish), Arpad (located south of Calno), and Hamath (located south of Arpad).

According to verse 11, Yahweh, the God of Israel, was an idol just like any other idol, as far as Assyria was concerned. But Assyria will be punished for this attitude, as verse 12 indicates. *I have removed boundaries of people* means that Assyria boasts about conquering nations and removing their people into exile.

Verse 15 contains two rhetorical questions that presuppose the answer *no*. No, an axe does not have power over the person who uses it, nor does a saw have more power than its user. Neither does Assyria have power over God, because God is using Assyria as an instrument of destruction.

Verses 16 through 19 are a series of images, describing what God will ultimately do to Assyria. We see God as a fire that will burn Assyria like a forest. We see Assyria as a stout warrior who will become wasted by a devastating sickness. The message is clear: God will protect the chosen people by wreaking havoc upon their enemies.

Remnant of Israel (10:20-23)

Although God will bring destruction on Judah, a remnant *(the suvivors of the house of Jacob)* will return to inhabit Judah again. The Holy One of Israel is a common designation for God in Isaiah's oracles. (See 5:19; 31:1.)

A remnant will return (verse 21) is the name of the prophet's son (Shear-jashub, in Hebrew). See Isaiah 7:1-9. Here the emphasis is on the negative aspect of remnant. Of all the people of God, *only* a remnant will survive the destruction. There are as many people in Israel as there are grains of sand in the sea. This fulfills the promise God gave to Jacob in Genesis 28:13-14. It also makes the threatened destruction all the more devastating, since it will involve so many people.

Oracle of Promise (10:24-27)

This oracle is directed to the people of Judah, *the ones who dwell in Zion.* They should trust God completely. Yes, there will be devastation at the hands of the Assyrians. But the time will come when the Assyrians themselves will be destroyed. That battle is described in terms of an earlier battle with the Midianites (see Judges 7), and in terms of the victory over the Egyptians at the Red Sea (Exodus 13–14).

The Assyrian Threat (10:28-34)

These verses describe an enemy march southward into the city of Jerusalem. The march begins in Rimmon, about twenty miles north of Jerusalem. From there the way proceeds southward, through Aiath (the city of Ai; see Joshua 8), and Migron, and stops temporarily at Michmash. Then the army crosses the pass (a wadi near

Michmash) and spends the night at Geba.

The second half of verse 29 and all of verse 30 describe panic among the cities surrounding Jerusalem, at the news of the advancing enemy. Panic reigns in Gallim, Laishah, and Anathoth. (See the glossary and map of Palestine for the location of these towns.)

Verses 31 and 32 describe the flight of the people when the enemy reaches Jerusalem. Madmenah and Gebim are located just outside Jerusalem's city gates. Verses 33 and 34 describe God's destruction of Assyria as a woodsman cuts down trees in a forest.

The Messianic King (11:1-9)

Chapter 11 discusses the messiah as the one who will bring about future salvation. Verses 1-9 describe the messianic king in language similar to that in Chapter 9.

The messiah is described as a shoot that will grow out of *the stump of Jesse,* who is the father of King David (see 1 Samuel 16). This image places the future messiah in the Davidic line. The messiah will have various gifts that will enable him to rule wisely: wisdom, understanding, counsel, might, knowledge, and fear of the Lord. Fear of God refers to obedience, or good behavior.

Verses 3-5 expand on the idea of ruling wisely by describing how this king will make judgments during his rule. He will judge with righteousness. In so doing he will be the champion of the poor and lowly. He will be able to smite those who do evil by his words alone.

Faithfulness (will be) *the girdle of his loins,* worn as his innermost layer of clothing so it remains close to him.

Verses 6-9 describe an idyllic future life that will be free from danger, brought about by the messianic king's rule of peace. Beasts that are normally enemies will live side-by-side in a peaceful manner. Verse 6 says *and a little child shall lead them.* If a young child can supervise a group of animals such as the ones listed, the situation must be peaceful. Verse 9 quotes Isaiah 65:25.

The Messianic Age (11:10-16)

This section expands on verses 1-9. The opening words *in that day* indicate that a new section begins here.

The *root of Jesse* refers to the messianic king, who will be acknowledged by all peoples at some future time.

Verses 11-16 describe Israel when the restoration has taken place. First of all, God will go to Israel's enemies and gather together the Israelites who remain in exile. This gathered people will become the remnant of Israel. *Yet a second time* refers to the first deliverance God accomplished on Israel's behalf, the Exodus from Egypt.

God will gather these people from Assyria, Egypt, Pathros (Northern Egypt), Ethiopia, Elam (to the east), Shinar (another name for Babylonia), and from Hamath (in Syria, north of Israel). All these places are countries except Hamath, which is a city. Perhaps the prophet chose Hamath rather than Syria in general because there was a large group of Israelites living there.

The *jealousy of Ephraim* (verse 13) refers to the broken relationship between Israel (Ephraim) and Judah, especially during the time of the Syro-Ephraimitic War (see the comments on Isaiah 7:1-9). Together Israel and Judah will stand against outside enemies; their first target will be Philistia, on the Mediterranean seacoast. From there, the combined armies will move eastward to Moab, Edom, and Ammon. All these territories are located on the eastern side of the Jordan River and the Dead Sea.

The *tongue of the Sea of Egypt* (verse 15) refers to the Red Sea. *The River* refers to the Euphrates River, in Mesopotamia. The *highway from Assyria* is an image found also in the later portion of Isaiah, when the prophet speaks of a highway on which the exiles will travel home to Judah.

A Song of Deliverance (12:1-3)

This song begins as an address from prophet to people, a promise that the people will someday be in a position to sing songs of praise. In effect, the prophet is putting words of praise into the mouth of the people. His words for them continue through the end of verse 2. The second half of verse 2 is reminiscent of some of the language found in the Psalms (see Psalm 118:14, for example).

Verse 3 mentions drawing *water from the wells of salvation*. Possibly this is a reference to a procession that took place during one of the festivals, and that went from the pool of Siloam to the courtyard of the Temple. Especially in this context, water represents life itself, a restored life for God's people.

A Song of Thanksgiving (12:4-6)

The first part of verse 4 echoes the first words of Miriam's song in Exodus 15. Now, God dwells in the midst of the people. This song of thanksgiving is sung in anticipation of a future restoration of the people of God.

§ § § § § § §

The Message of Isaiah 10–12

§ God's people have been disobedient. God will not hesitate to punish them, nor will God hesitate to restore them again in the future.

§ God intends to use Assyria as an instrument to bring about the destruction of Judah.

§ God sent Isaiah to harden the hearts of the people, in order to bring about their repentance and restoration.

§ God will watch over the people by (ultimately) destroying their enemies.

§ God will use the future messianic king to bring about justice, righteousness, and an era of peace. This king will depend on God for support in his mission.

§ § § § § § §

Isaiah 13–16

Introduction to These Chapters

These four chapters begin the second major section of the Book of Isaiah, Chapters 13–28. These chapters contain mainly Isaiah's oracles concerning foreign nations.
Here is an outline of Chapters 13–16.

- I. Oracle Against Babylon (13:1-22)
  - A. God summons the armies (13:1-5)
  - B. The day of the Lord (13:6-16)
  - C. God stirs up the Medes (13:17-22)
- II. Oracle Against Babylon's King (14:1-23)
  - A. Return from exile (14:1-2)
  - B. Taunt song to Babylon's king (14:3-23)
- III. Oracle Against Assyria (14:24-27)
- IV. Oracle Against Philistia (14:28-32)
- V. Oracle Against Moab (15:1–16:14)
  - A. Raid on Moab (15:1-9)
  - B. Fate of the Moabites (16:1-5)
  - C. Destruction of Moab (16:6-14)

Oracle Against Babylon (13:1-22)

This section speaks in detail and with vivid imagery about the destruction of the Babylonian empire. For the prophet Isaiah, this event would have been about 200 years in the future (538 B.C.). Consequently, most scholars date at least parts of these oracles sometime soon after the fall of Babylon and the rise to power of Cyrus, King of Persia (538 B.C.).

God Summons the Armies (13:1-5)

This section is introduced by a prophetic formula which names the prophet Isaiah, son of Amoz, as the recipient of the oracle. The formula is similar to those used in Isaiah 1:1 and 2:1. This heading makes the point that the oracles against foreign nations, in Chapters 13–39, come from Isaiah just as the oracles in Chapters 1–12 did.

Rather than using the word *vision*, this introductory formula uses *oracle*. However, the translation of this word is disputed. Some translations use *burden* (following the Latin Vulgate); others translate the word as a raising of the voice, or an *oracle*.

Verses 2-3 describe the preparation for attack. At the beginning of verse 2 it is unclear who is speaking. On a hill overlooking the city of Babylon a signal will be raised, as a sign of the time to attack. Jeremiah 51:12, 27 speaks of a *standard* that is used in a similar way. It is now time, according to the speaker, to enter the gates of the city. In verse 3 we begin to see that the commander of these armies is none other than God.

In verse 4 our attention is directed toward the mountains overlooking the city. The armies are gathering together in preparation for battle. Here in verse 4 the address changes from first person (God speaking) to a third person narrative about God's actions. Verse 5 indicates that God gathers armies from all over the world (the Babylonian empire).

The Day of the Lord (13:6-16)

In this section the day of the Lord is seen as the time when Babylon will be destroyed. Whereas in earlier prophecies the day of the Lord was seen as a time of God's judgment on Israel and Judah (see Amos 8:9-10, for example), here that time is seen as a time of judgment on Israel's enemies.

The nature of the battle being waged changes in this section, from an attack on the city of Babylon to a cataclysmic confrontation that will *make the earth a desolation* (verse 9). Terrible things will happen at that time, as described in verses 7-10. People will be paralyzed with fear. They will be doubled over in pain. The whole earth will be clothed in darkness, because the sun, moon, and stars will shed no light.

In verse 10 God speaks in the first person. In the description of judgment that follows, almost no one escapes. Those who will are *more rare than fine gold*.

Verse 13 describes the shaking of the earth's foundations because of the voice of God. A similar image is found in Amos 9:1-4.

Verses 14-16 portray with vivid imagery what life will be like when the day of the Lord comes. People will be confused and will try to find their own homes. But their attempts will be unsuccessful, for they will be like sheep without a shepherd. They will run aimlessly. They will die if encountered by an attacker. Their children will be killed, their wives raped, and their homes destroyed. The picture painted here is one of total destruction.

God Stirs Up the Medes (13:17-22)

The word *Behold*, which begins verse 17, indicates the start of a new section. Here the Medes are described as led by God in an attack on Babylon. The Medes were a people who lived northwest of Persia, and who allied with Babylon to defeat the Assyrians. These Medes are summoned by God, apparently, to carry out acts of cruelty against the inhabitants of the city. Verse 18 is difficult to translate, and the English version appearing in any given translation is a guess at best.

Verse 19 draws a sharp contrast between the Babylon of the present (in the writer's time) and the Babylon of the future. A city that is now glorious will then be desolate, a dwelling place for wild animals. *Chaldeans* is another name for Babylonians. Sodom and Gomorrah are examples of cities that have received similar judgments (see Genesis 19). No nomad will settle in the ruined city, even temporarily.

Verse 21 mentions that both animals and goat demons (satyrs) will dwell in Babylon. Several other prophetic passages speak of judgment upon a city in a similar way. See Zephaniah 2:14-16 (judgment on Nineveh), Isaiah 34:10-15 (judgment on Edom), and Jeremiah 50:35-40 (judgment on Babylon). Revelation 18:2-3 speaks of the future of Babylon in a similar way.

Verse 22 is echoed in other prophetic texts such as Ezekiel 7:7, Obadiah 15, Jeremiah 48:16, and Joel 1:15.

Return From Exile (14:1-2)

This short section assures the people of Judah that God will have compassion on Jacob and will again choose Israel. See Isaiah 49:13 for a similar image. *Aliens will join them* refers to non-Israelites who felt motivated to join with the Israelites. Verse 2 specifies what will happen after the return from exile. Rather than being the slaves of their captors, the Israelites will enslave those who were once their captors, a complete reversal of their former situation. Verse 2 is reminiscent of the imagery used in the Book of Exodus, when the slavery in Egypt was described (see Exodus 1). This same idea is expressed in Isaiah 49:22-26.

Taunt Song to Babylon's King (14:3-23)

Verses 3-23 are a dirge, or lament, against a tyrant who is identified as the *King of Babylon* (verse 4). The prophet does not say which king the song refers to. He speaks to the people in verse 3, indicating that they should sing the song to the Babylonian king. This verse and the first half of verse 4 introduce the taunt song, which begins in the second half of verse 4.

Verses 4-8 indicate that peace and rest will reign on the earth when the king of Babylon is subdued. In these verses, the scene described takes place on the earth; the situation changes at verse 9. The Revised Standard Version translates the last phrase in verse 4 as *the insolent fury ceased*, but the meaning of the Hebrew is uncertain.

The message of verses 5-6 is similar to that of Isaiah 10:5-6: God will punish the enemies of Israel. Verse 8 mentions the *cypresses* and the *cedars of Lebanon*. These are references to the fact that the Babylonians, in their campaign against Syria/Palestine, plundered the wealth of the forests in the northern part of the region. They used the wood to build their own buildings in their own lands.

Verses 9-11 describe the circumstances surrounding the death of this tyrant. He will join former rulers in the region of Sheol, where all persons are reduced to the status of mere shadows. *Sheol* is another word for the underworld. It was thought to be located underneath the cosmic sea that the earth rested upon. Sheol is often described as a pit, or cistern, especially in the Psalms (see Psalm 88:3-4, for example).

The prophet uses vivid imagery here. The former rulers, now in the form of shadows, sit waiting for the king to arrive. When he does, they ridicule him, accusing him of receiving the same fate that they did.

Verses 12-15 describe the failure of the tyrant to ascend into heaven. *Day Star* and *Son of Dawn* are translations of names of Canaanite deities, as is *Most High* (in verse 14). Genesis 14:19 uses the same designation. The message of these verses is that this tyrant, this ruler of Babylon, is destined to be brought down to Sheol as a judgment on his plans to rule over the nations.

Verses 16-20 continue the description of the humiliation, describing his ultimate fate. In death, he will not even have the dignity of being buried in a grave, a fate most repulsive in Old Testament culture. *Like a loathed untimely birth* could also be translated *like a loathed branch*, following one variant Hebrew version.

Not only will this ruler not be buried, his name will not endure on earth through his descendants. His sons will be slaughtered because of his own sins. A similar fate befell King Zedekiah when Jerusalem fell in 587 B.C. (See 2 Kings 25.) Verses 22 and 23 re-emphasize that the nation of Babylon will be utterly destroyed. Unlike the nation of Israel, Babylon will leave no remnant, not a trace.

Oracle Against Assyria (14:24-27)

The prophet speaks similar words against Assyria in 17:12-14; 30:7-33; and 37:22-29. The message of this section is that God will deal one final blow to Assyria. Once God has decided to punish Assyria, nothing can change this decision (*As I have planned, so shall it be*).

Oracle Against Philistia (14:28-32)

This speech is dated *in the year that King Ahaz died*, or 715 B.C. This introduction is similar to the introduction to the prophet's call in Chapter 6. The image of the *broken rod* is used in Chapter 9.

The message is clear and inescapable. The Philistines should not be complacent regarding their own security. Although it appears that they are safe, God will smite all of them, even their remnant. Verse 30 is difficult to translate, for it alternates between first person address and third person address. Most translations use one or the other (the RSV uses first-person in both places).

Raid on Moab (15:1-9)

These verses describe a nighttime attack on Moab. The enemy is not named. The description is given in the form of a lament, which becomes clear if the poem is read aloud. The 3 + 2 meter indicates the lament form. *Because AR-is laid waste-in a night---Moab-is undone.*

Up to the high places refers to open spaces on the tops of hills where altars were built and cultic rituals took place.

Verses 2-3 describe a time of mourning, when the men shave their heads and beards, and put on sackcloth.

*Heshbon and Elealeh—two Moabite cities—cry out, either

because they have heard the bad news or because they themselves have been affected. All the locations mentioned in verses 5-9 are in the territory of Moab, east of the Jordan River. In verse 9, the town of Dimon is mentioned. Following some versions, the RSV translates the word as Dibon. However, it is possible that Dimon and Dibon are two separate locations.

The Fate of The Moabites (16:1-5)

They at the beginning of verse 1 refers to the Moabites, who have sent men to the ruler of the conquering nation, asking for refuge. *Sela* means rock; *the rock of the desert* is an unknown location.

Destruction of Moab (16:6-14)

This section is paralleled in Jeremiah 48:29-33. It uses the 3+2 meter of the lament. *The raisin-cakes* of Kir-Hareseth refer to the process of wine production, which has now been halted due to the destruction of the countryside. The *vine of Sibmah* refers to a town located near Heshbon, and Jazer is another (unidentified) Moabite town.

§ § § § § § §

The Message of Isaiah 13–16

§ God uses other nations as instruments to bring about the ultimate fate of the people of Israel/Judah.

§ The power and might of a foreign nation does not always assure its position as a leader.

§ Ultimate doom is not in store for Israel, as long as the people recognize the absolute authority of God.

§ The suffering Israel had to endure was for the ultimate goal of restoration as the people of God.

§ § § § § § §

Isaiah 17–20

Introduction to These Chapters

Chapters 17–20 continue the theme of oracles against foreign nations. Most of the speeches in this section focus on Egypt (Chapters 18–20). These oracles concerning Egypt are preceded by an oracle against Damascus and a warning against idolatry.

Here is an outline of Chapters 17–20.

The Fate of Damascus (17:1-3)

The fact that Ephraim, or Israel, is mentioned in verse 3 dates this oracle to the time of the Syro-Ephraimitic War, in 734–732 B.C. (See the commentary on Isaiah 7 for a fuller discussion of this historical period.) Pekah, king of Israel (Ephraim) and Rezin, king of Syria, allied themselves against King Ahaz of Judah, in an effort to force him into a alliance against Assyria. King Ahaz, against the advice of the prophet Isaiah, paid tribute to Tiglath-Pileser III, the Assyrian king.

In response, the Assyrians conquered Damascus, the capital of Assyria, in 732 B.C., and Samaria, the capital of Israel, in 721 B.C. That historical background helps to explain the prophecy in verse 3: Ephraim (Israel) and Syria will both be defeated. Damascus, an important city in the political arena, *will cease to be a city*. The destruction will be so complete that shepherds will be able to pasture their flocks there.

The Fate of Jacob (17:4-6)

These verses continue the description of what will happen to Syria (Damascus). *In that day* signals the introduction of a new thought. *Jacob* symbolizes the Northern Kingdom, which is destined to lose its *glory*, its respect and power among the nations. The prophet uses the image of a man formerly fat, who has grown thin as a result of the devastation.

Verse 5 uses an image taken from agriculture. When *the reaper gathers standing grain*, he uses his left arm to gather the grain and his right arm to cut off the ears of corn with a sickle. (See also Jeremiah 50:16.) When this process is taking place, the reaper wants as few ears left standing as possible. That will be the situation with the people of Judah. Few people will remain standing. The *valley of Rephaim* is located just northwest of the city of Jerusalem.

Verse 6 elaborates on the idea of just a few persons left standing. After an olive tree is harvested, the only fruit left remaining will be found on the uppermost branches. When the harvest is plentiful, what is left in the top of the trees is almost nothing.

The People Will Turn to God (17:7-9)

Again, the words *on that day* begin verse 7 indicating that a new thought is being introduced. The time being referred to is the end of time, when the final judgment will occur. A contrast is made between God, the Holy One of Israel (a common designation for God in Isaiah's prophecies) and the idols that represent the Canaanite religion. At that time people will forsake these idols, made with their own hands, and will turn to God as the true source of their own salvation.

Verse 9 introduces still another idea. The destruction that will take place will leave the cities desolate. The Hivites and the Amorites were people who inhabited the area of Palestine before the Israelites invaded the territory under the leadership of Joshua, some 500 years earlier. There will be no other people to take their place.

Punishment for Idolatry (17:10-11)

Verse 10 addresses a group of unidentified persons (the word *you* is singular, but the addressee is meant to personify a group of people). The wording of these verses sounds similar to the language of some of the psalms. Whoever is being addressed is accused of having forgotten God, as shown by the practice of idol worship. Planting and nurturing will bring no harvest, just as death and destruction will come to the people.

A Storm Brews (17:12-14)

These verses describe a terrible storm that will descend upon the land, bringing roaring thunder and high winds. Perhaps the reference is to the assault on Jerusalem in the time of Hezekiah (701 B.C.), by the invading Assyrian armies. The city of Jerusalem has nothing to fear from this storm, however. God will protect the people against the onslaught (verse 13).

Verse 13 uses another image from the agricultural world. Ears of corn are ground up together with their sheaves. The mixture is then thrown into the wind, causing the chaff to dissipate and the usable grain to drop to the ground. In a similar way, the Assyrians will be chased away.

First Oracle Against Egypt (18:1-7)

The background of this oracle seems to be the attempt at formation of an alliance with Egypt against the Assyrian threat (about 714 B.C.). *Land of whirring wings* refers to Ethiopia, a territory south of Egypt. The image portrayed is of ambassadors coming down the Nile River in boats made of papyrus. The *land the rivers divide* is Egypt, divided by the Nile.

The message of verse 4 is important. Whatever happens among the nations on earth, God will be remote and detached. But then, at a time when God is ready, the revolt will begin. The prophet uses the metaphor of the harvest to indicate God's decision about when the time is right. God will act *when the flower becomes a ripening grape* (verse 5). In the land of the prophet (Palestine), blossoms begin to appear on the grape vines in the spring. By the end of August the grapes have ripened, and in September they are harvested.

What message are the messengers supposed to convey? Egypt, a world power, will be destroyed. Then the inhabitants of that country will be subject to God. They will bring gifts to God, who dwells in Mount Zion, in Jerusalem.

Second Oracle Against Egypt (19:1-15)

This oracle is divided into three parts. The first part (verses 1-4) describes the chaos that will result (in Egypt) after God's judgment on the people. The second part (verses 5-10) describes the collapse of Egypt's economy, and the third part (verses 10-15) portrays the reaction of the king and his advisors to what is happening to the nation.

The civil chaos described in verses 1-4 might possibly have resulted from the inauguration of a new dynasty in Egypt in 714 B.C. In verse 1, God is on the way to Egypt, *riding on a swift cloud.* Verse 2 explains what God intends to accomplish there. The people will fight among themselves, and cities will also do battle with each other. They will lose their sense of national pride. They will become confused and begin to turn to sorcery to help them figure out what to do. In other words, God intends to confuse them into inaction.

In verse 4 we see the particulars of God's intentions. God will turn the Egyptians over to *the hand of a hard master* (a foreign ruler).

Verses 5-10 describe the collapse of the Egyptian economy, brought about initially by drought. The Nile River was absolutely essential to the existence of Egypt. Drying up that river would make an immediate impact, putting an end to the fertility of the nation. All persons whose livelihood depends on agriculture will be distressed.

Verses 11-15 discuss the reaction of the king and his advisors. *Zoan* is an Egyptian city located in the northeastern delta region. The prophet describes Egypt's leaders as stupid and foolish. He then begins to taunt them, telling them they should have understood God's purposes all along.

Verse 15 summarizes the situation presented in verses 1-15. Egypt will not be able to act in any meaningful way. *Head or tail, palm branch or reed* echoes Isaiah 9:14. *Palm branch and reed* refer to those who rule and those who are ruled. *Head or tail* means no part of the country.

Conversion of Egypt and Assyria (19:16-25)

This section consists of five subsections, each beginning with the words *in that day. That day* in the first section (verses 16-17) refers to the time when God will bring about the disaster described in the previous section (verses 1-15). The Egyptians will be so terrorized that they will tremble visibly.

The second subsection consists of verse 18, which opens with the formula *in that day.* This section mentions five Egyptian cities that will *speak the language of Canaan*

(Hebrew) and will worship the God of Israel. The prophet is probably referring to Jewish settlements in Egypt that he is aware of. He mentions only one by name—City of the Sun (Heliopolis). The fact that these cities are established within Egypt indicates that the day of judgment on Egypt is approaching.

Verses 19-22 form the third subsection. These verses make clear how the Egyptians will know that it is Israel's God at work. An altar will be built to God inside the nation of Egypt. The Egyptians will respond by worshiping God at that altar with sacrifices and burnt offerings. This conversion of the Egyptians will result in God's hearing their supplications. Thus God is portrayed as both smiter and healer.

Verse 23 also opens with the words *in that day*. It speaks of a highway that runs from Egypt to Syria. Along this highway, Egyptians and Assyrians will travel back and forth to each other's countries, where they will worship each other's gods.

Verses 24 and 25 make up the last subsection in the larger section on the conversion of Egypt and Assyria. Three nations will be blessed by God when this conversion takes place: Egypt, Assyria, and Israel. All these people together will be the new people of God.

Third Oracle Against Egypt (20:1-6)

This short section is more like a narrative than an oracle. It is written in prose rather than poetry. The historical background of these events is an alliance between the Egyptian Pharaoh (Shabako) and the leaders in Judah against the Assyrians, sometime around 715 B.C. Ashdod was one of the cities in Palestine involved in defending the territory against the Assyrian threat.

When reading this section it is best to consider verse 2 as a kind of parenthetical statement. Its message is that God told Isaiah to behave as he did, not the prophet himself or anyone else.

Verse 3 indicates that Isaiah's nakedness gives a message to Egypt that the Assyrian threat is imminent. When the Assyrian army finishes its work, many persons will be without clothes and shoes.

The inhabitants of this coastland (verse 6) are those who dwell in Ashdod and the surrounding cities of Philistia (on the coast of the Mediterranean Sea).

§ § § § § § §

The Message of Isaiah 17–20

Most of the material in these four chapters focuses on the nation of Egypt, and what will happen to that nation at some time in the future. What do these oracles tell us about Israel's God? about the people of Israel? about Egypt?

§ God's judgment on sin and disobedience extends far beyond the limits of God's own people. God will punish other nations as well.

§ Because God is active in history, we can never be certain of the future. Nor can we control it.

§ God will not act in history until the time is right. God can be a spectator of historical events if that is appropriate in God's eyes.

§ God will listen to supplications made not only by the people of Israel, but by the people of other nations as well. God has the power to change the course of history.

§ § § § § § §

Isaiah 21–23

Introduction to These Chapters

This section begins with an oracle against Babylon, followed by messages to other nations such as Edom, Arabia, and Sidon (a city). Isaiah 21–23 concludes a larger section of the book (Chapters 13–23) in which most of the prophet's oracles against foreign nations are contained.

Here is an outline of Chapters 21–23.

  I. Oracle Against Babylon (21:1-10)
 II. Oracle Against Edom (21:11-12)
III. Oracle Against Arabia (21:13-17)
 IV. Warning to Jerusalem (22:1-14)
  V. Oracle Against Shebna (22:15-25)
 VI. Oracle Against Tyre and Sidon (23:1-18)

Oracle Against Babylon (21:1-10)

Much of this oracle is difficult to interpret, beginning with the first phrase in verse 1, *the wilderness of the sea*. Most commentators think the word *sea* is a textual error. They omit that word, leaving the introduction *Oracle concerning the wilderness*. The rest of verse 1, which continues to introduce the oracle, describes in vivid imagery the imminent arrival of the message. The words are coming like a whirlwind sweeping through the desert, causing sand to blow like a sandstorm.

All at once in verse 2 the tone changes. Now the prophet assumes a serious attitude, delivering the message in as few words as possible. The attackers are identified as Elamites and Medes. Elam is a country located east of

Babylon. Media, home of the Medes, is also located east of Babylon, north of Elam. At the end of verse 2 we realize that God is speaking, the God who resolves to *bring to a end* all the sighing. This sighing could be the whole creation or it could be the people of Judah.

Verses 3 through 5 predict judgment through destruction. God is in agony, even to the point of experiencing pain like the pain of labor. The twilight hour, which is the most pleasant time of day in that part of the world, does not bring its expected relief (from the heat of the day). Instead, God trembles in anguish. Why?

Verse 5 makes the reason clear. The people in the city, instead of repenting and resolving to take their situation seriously, are drinking and eating and carousing. *They prepare the table* could mean one of two things. Either the military leaders of Babylon just sit down to a feast and are interrupted by a call to arms, or Babylon is being compared to a table set and ready for a feast (attack). *Oil the shield* means prepare the leather shields to increase their flexibility and make them more usable in battle.

In verses 6-9, God commands the prophet to set a watchman out who will announce when the armies have arrived. When this watchman sees pairs of horses with riders, donkeys, and camels approaching, he is to announce their arrival. Verse 9 then repeats the watchman's announcement. The army has arrived. The description of what he sees is slightly different from what he was to look for; he sees horses with riders only, no donkeys or camels. To this announcement God answers: *Fallen, fallen is Babylon*. This language imitates the laments used at funerals in ancient times. Amos 5:2 uses similar language to describe the downfall of Israel. In verse 10 the prophet speaks again, concluding the oracle.

Oracle Against Edom (21:11-12)

This short passage is difficult to understand and interpret. Verse 11 opens with the introduction *The oracle concerning Dumah.* The identification of Dumah is uncertain. It could be a variation of the name *Edom* (thus the heading of this section). Dumah could also refer to a town in Arabia, east of Edom. Or, the word could be translated *silence,* and its symbolic reference be to Edom.

Verse 11 describes a watchman, in a unknown location, being questioned by a impatient Edomite about when the morning light will come. (*Seir* is a mountain range in Edom.) In order to hear Edomites calling him, this watchman must have been standing on the east side of southern Judah, on the border between Judah and Edom. This oracle has a symbolic meaning. Darkness or night, symbolizing disaster or chaos, will give way to light, or salvation, only when the time is right.

Oracle Against Arabia (21:13-17)

This oracle is introduced in verse 13 by the words *the oracle concerning Arabia.* It is addressed to a group of *Dedanites,* who are from the northern region of Arabia. These persons are told to make their settlements in the thickets, rather than along the main caravan routes. If they obey this command, the Dedanites will deprive themselves of water, causing themselves and their animals to risk dying of thirst. So, *the inhabitants of the land of Tema* (near Dedan) are commanded to bring them food and water. Apparently these Dedanites are fleeing from some battle in which they have been defeated.

Kedan (also in northern Arabia) will be destroyed within three years, according to the conclusion of this oracle.

Warning to Jerusalem (22:1-14)

The formulas used at the beginning (*The oracle concerning the valley of vision*) and at the end (*says the Lord God of hosts*) of this oracle are standard formulas used to mark off prophetic speeches. This oracle is related historically to the invasion of Jerusalem by King Sennacherib of Assyria, in 701 B.C.

The *valley of vision* (verse 1) is mentioned also in verse 5. Perhaps this is another name for the valley of Hinnom, located just outside Jerusalem's walls.

Verses 2 and 3 describe a city that has just gone through an invasion by enemy armies and has come out on the other side. The survivors have gone up onto the rooftops and are shouting with joy (because the battle is over). At the same time, they have been abandoned by their rulers, who surrendered to the enemy. God is angered by a similar attitude in 21:5.

The prophet speaks (verse 4). He is horrified by what he sees. People are shouting for joy when *the daughter of my people* (Jerusalem) has been decimated.

Verses 5-8 describe the coming day of the Lord as a day of utter confusion. Walls will tumble down and armies will invade the city. Elam is a territory in Mesopotamia. Kir is a city in Moab, east of the Dead Sea. *The covering of Judah* (verse 8) probably refers to the protection God had formerly given, which was now being taken away.

In verses 9-11, the prophet accuses the people in Jerusalem of looking for military fortifications when they should have called upon God for help. *The House of the Forest* refers to the royal palace in Jerusalem, perhaps the same one that was originally built by Solomon. Evidently, the people collected weapons, repaired the wall using stones from houses, collected a water supply, and made a reservoir for water storage. They did all these things but did not ask God, *who planned it long ago,* for help.

Verses 12-14 speak of Jerusalem's guilt in the eyes of the prophet. The people did not realize that God was calling for repentance. Their reaction was, instead, *let us eat and drink,* for tomorrow we die. Verse 14 makes the punishment clear. They will not be forgiven, ever.

Oracle Against Shebna (22:15-25)

Verses 15-16 accuse Shebna, a secretary in the court of King Hezekiah. Apparently, this official had attempted to seize for himself power and prestige by carving a tomb for himself in an improper location. The judgment is announced in verses 17-25. God will send him to a wide land (perhaps Assyria), where he will die.

According to verse 20, Eliakim will replace Shebna in the court of Hezekiah. Shebna's robe and girdle signify the authority of the office, which is now being given over to Eliakim. He will have the keys to the house of David (palace). That he will be the one to decide when the doors open and shut also signifies high authority. In verse 25, however, we see that Eliakim would become a disappointment, just as his predecessor was.

Oracle Against Tyre and Sidon (23:1-18)

The address in this oracle alternates between Tyre and Sidon. Some commentators believe that two previously separate speeches have been woven together into a combined oracle. Verses 1-4, 12-14 are addressed to Sidon; verses 5-11, 15-18 are addressed to Tyre. The meter in most of the chapter is the 3 + 2 meter of the lament.

After the introduction, verse 1 continues with *Wail, O ships of Tarshish*. This phrase is repeated as a kind of refrain toward the end of the poem (verse 14). *Ships of Tarshish is a phrase used to describe merchant vessels that were especially seaworthy (see 1 Kings 22:48). The city of Tarshish is usually mentioned as a far-away place. The message is: Tyre has been abandoned.*

Verse 2 addresses the inhabitants of the coast (those who dwell in Tyre and Sidon, cities on the Mediterranean seacoast). *The grain of Shihor* refers to the harvest that comes from the region of northeastern Egypt. Sidon, which was once the *merchant of the nations,* is now silent.

According to verse 4, Sidon is now childless because its inhabitants have been slain in battle.

Verse 6 addresses a lament to *the inhabitants of the coast.* The question in verse 7 emphasizes how far these cities have fallen. Verse 8 asks who is responsible for the fate of Tyre, and verse 9 answers the question. God wanted to humble the city's inhabitants.

Verses 10-14 describe the situation that now exists in the city of Tyre. There is no escape from God's power. There would be no point trying to build up a merchant fleet again. The sea will no longer cooperate. Even if the inhabitants of Sidon flee to Cyprus, they will not escape.

Verses 15-18 describe a destruction of Tyre *at the end of seventy years*. Most commentators see this section as a later addition, reflecting the siege of Alexander the Great on Tyre in 332 B.C. The writer mocks Tyre with a song that might have been sung by a harlot in the streets (verse 16). Seventy years should not be taken literally; it refers to one life span. (See Psalm 90:10, where a life span is said to be threescore and ten years.)

In that day, those who survive the attack will make a pilgrimage to Jerusalem to pay homage to God. Their merchandise, which at one time made them so prosperous, will now be dedicated to God.

§ § § § § § §

The Message of Isaiah 21–23

§ God acts for the purpose of calling the people to repentance. When they do not respond appropriately, God will punish them again.

§ There can be no rest, no escape from God's judgment, until there is trust in God.

§ God's judgment can come upon foreign nations just as it comes upon God's own people. Final judgment will involve everyone.

§ Fortifications and an abundance of weapons cannot compensate for a failure to trust in God.

§ § § § § § §

Isaiah 24–27

Introduction to These Chapters

Chapters 24–27 of the Book of Isaiah are usually called the *Isaiah Apocalypse.* Their content is primarily eschatological (relating to events at the end of time). Various kinds of prophetic literature are found in these chapters, such as apocalyptic poetry, eschatological prophecies, oracles of judgment, and oracles of salvation.

Here is an outline of Chapters 24–27.
  I. Total Destruction (24:1-13)
  II. Future Deliverance (24:14-16)
  III. Total Destruction (24:17-23)
  IV. Thanksgiving Song (25:1-5)
  V. Eschatological Oracles (25:6-12)
  VI. Victory Song (26:1-6)
  VII. Future Restoration (26:7-19)
  VIII. Future Judgment (26:20–27:1)
  IX. Future Deliverance (27:2-11)
  X. Concluding Oracle (27:12-13)

Most commentators agree that the Isaiah Apocalypse was not the work of the prophet Isaiah. Various suggestions have been made for the date of this section. Whereas the prophet Isaiah is most often concerned with the judgment God is about to bring upon Judah, the events spoken of in Chapters 24–27 are on a worldwide scale. Concern for the events that will take place at the end of time is characteristic of the theology of later Judaism, perhaps dating these chapters to 400 or 300 B.C.

Many of the prophecies in these chapters concern a certain city, whose identity is uncertain. Commentators have suggested such cities as Carthage, Babylon, and Samaria, but no one knows for certain. That is unfortunate, since the identification of the city might tell us something about the origin and date of these prophecies.

Total Destruction (24:1-13)

The first three verses in this section introduce the apocalypse as a whole, since they paint a picture of total destruction at a future time. The earth's surface will be twisted, and its inhabitants scattered far and wide. Possibly, the reference is to an earthquake. The destruction spoken of here is of the same scope as that described in the story of Noah (see Genesis 6–9). The pairs mentioned in verse two (master-slave, maid-mistress, and so forth) represent the totality of human beings. No one will escape destruction because of social status. Verse 3 sums up the message. *The earth shall be utterly laid waste,* because God has spoken *this word.*

Verses 4-6 give the reason for this judgment. Earth and heaven will wither due to a massive drought, because its inhabitants have sinned. They have *broken the everlasting covenant* (possibly the covenant with Noah in Genesis 9).

Verses 7-13 describe what the circumstances in the unnamed city will be like after the destruction. Those who were formerly happy will take to sighing. Musical instruments will not be played anymore. The people become too serious to drink wine, and stronger drink tastes better to them. Houses are shut up; people are generally depressed. The city gates have fallen down. According to verse 13, only a few people will survive the destruction and thus live in the desolate city. When an olive tree is beaten at harvest time, few olives are left. So it will be with the people of the city. (See also Isaiah 17:6.)

Future Deliverance (24:14-16)

These three verses describe a time of exultation that will follow the destruction. The people who have survived will sing songs of praise to God. It is unclear who is speaking in verses 15 and 16. Perhaps they are the Hebrew people who are joyful over other people worshiping their own God. The second half of verse 16 is difficult to understand; its tone connects it with verses 17-23 rather than verses 14-16.

Total Destruction (24:17-23)

Again the message is a promise of destruction and chaos. *The pit* is a metaphor for Sheol, the underworld. There is no escape from the terrors of death. *The windows of heaven* (verse 18) are openings in the firmament that let the rain through. If these are opened up, there will be no limit to the amount of rain that falls upon the earth. *The foundations of the earth* begin to shake, as in an earthquake. Amos 9:1-4 describes a similar catastrophe. Verse 20 portrays the earth staggering *like a drunken man* who has lost his equilibrium.

Verses 21-23 describe the end of this world and the beginning of the next world, the reign of God. The *host of heaven* are deities, or stars. The stars, along with earthly beings, will be gathered together in a pit (probably another reference to Sheol, the underworld). The light that will be provided in the reign of God on earth will be so bright that the sun will not be necessary and the moon will not be seen.

So we see in these three verses that judgment comes first, but then salvation. There is always hope for God's people. The rulers will be punished, and God will reign.

Thanksgiving Song (25:1-5)

In these verses an unidentified worshiper offers a song of thanksgiving for the fall of an unknown city. In its tone and language, this section sounds like Psalm 145.

The palace of aliens (verse 2) refers to the government represented in the city; it will no longer exist when God destroys the city. At that time, nations that are now strong will recognize God's power and will fear God.

Eschatological Oracles (25:6-12)

In this section, future salvation is described and celebrated for other nations as well as for Israel. *This mountain* means Mount Zion, in Jerusalem. At the future time of salvation, God will prepare a feast for all those who make pilgrimage to Jerusalem. The detailed description in verse 6 makes the point that the best possible feast will be prepared for the nations. The *covering,* or *veil,* mentioned in verse 7 presumably means the veil of mourning. The time of mourning will be over. That idea is reinforced in verse 8.

Verses 9-10 are a thanksgiving song, introduced by the formula *It will be said on that day.* The message of the song is that God will not disappoint those who have walked in hope. The second half of verse 10 draws a sharp contrast between Israel and Moab. Whereas Israel will live under God's protection, Moab will *be trodden down* as straw is in a dung pit. The reference to Moab is for one of two reasons. Either Moab is being singled out for judgment because of past sins (see Deuteronomy 23:3-6), or Moab represents Israel's enemies in a general way.

Victory Song (26:1-6)

The song contained in this section is one that would be sung by the people returning to Jerusalem after the final day of judgment has passed. Here we can be certain that the city mentioned in verse 1 is Jerusalem. *Open up the gates* (verse 2) is reminiscent of the language of the Psalms. Verses 3 and 4 indicate that trust in God is the characteristic attitude of those who will return to Zion in that day.

Verses 5 and 6 give reasons for the praise given to God. God has exalted the faithful and humbled the unfaithful. The footsteps of the *poor and needy* have trampled the unfaithful into the ground. This section as a whole (verses 1-6) conveys an important message: Trust in God, and you will survive the final judgment and return to Jerusalem to worship God in joy and triumph.

Future Restoration (26:7-19)

This lengthy section continues the theme of the future restoration of the people of God. Again using the language of the Psalms, the poet begins this section with an expression of confidence in God. God will make the way of the righteous level and smooth; there is nothing to fear. Whatever judgments God makes will be for the best, according to verse 8.

Verse 10 expands on the contrast between the fate of the righteous and the wicked (a theme often heard in the Psalms and the wisdom literature). The wicked should not be treated favorably because they will never learn to change their ways. They will never learn to trust God. Verse 11 refers to those who, in their spiritual blindness, do not recognize the hand of God in what happens to them. They will be judged for their stubbornness, in the end.

Verse 12 expresses the confidence that the supplication to God will be heard. After all, God has done wonderful things on behalf of the people in the past. For that reason, God is recognized as above the power and influence of all other gods and all earthly rulers. In the end, God is the only ruler to be acknowledged, remembered, and worshiped.

Verses 16-19 begin with a lament addressed directly to God, and composed in a 3+2 meter. When the people thought they were without God, they *poured out a prayer* asking for help. Their agony is compared to a woman in labor. However, whereas a woman in labor brings forth a child, these people bring forth only *wind*. They are helpless themselves, and unable to help the nation.

Verse 19 draws a contrast to what precedes. Although the people appear to be dead, they will be raised from the dust to sing for joy. God's light will illuminate them and their circumstances, and they will respond in praise and thanksgiving.

Future Judgment (26:20–27:1)

Now future judgment is described again. The people are called to go into their houses, shut their doors, and hide inside *for a little while* until God's anger abates. Verse 21 describes what God's wrath, which will last only a short time, will be like. The description is of God rushing down upon the city without warning, to punish those who are guilty.

Chapter 27 begins with a promise that *in that day* God will not only punish the guilty, but will bring judgment on Leviathan, who represents God's enemies. Leviathan was a sea monster in Canaanite mythology. Verse 1 also mentions a *dragon* that lives in the sea, which is another sea monster. Some commentators understand the two references to Leviathan and one reference to the sea monster as symbolizing three enemies of God and Israel. Others see the *fleeing* serpent and the *twisting* serpent as references to rivers, such as the Nile, Tigris, and Euphrates.

Future Deliverance (27:2-11)

This song about a vineyard is in contrast to the song of the vineyard found in Isaiah 5:1-7. Verse 2 forms the introduction to the song, using the familiar words *in that day*. Verse 3 indicates that God is speaking in the first person. Rather than destroying the vineyard (as in Isaiah 5:5-6), God will protect the vineyard from outside harm. God will water this vineyard (verse 3), rather than commanding the clouds not to rain on it (see 5:6).

According to verse 4, God is not angry with the yield of this vineyard. There are no thorns and briars to battle. As a result, this vineyard will not be destroyed. As far as outside enemies are concerned (nations other than Israel, the vineyard), they will need to make peace with God. The repetition in verse 5 is for emphasis.

Israel and Jacob will, at some time in the future, blossom again. At that time the original promise made to Abraham will be fulfilled (see Genesis 12:1-3).

Verse 7 asks a rhetorical question which expects a negative response. No, God has not treated Israel in the same way as Israel's enemies were treated. God's punishment has been harsher on other nations. The *east wind* refers to the Sirocco, a hot, dry wind that sweeps through the desert. Although God punished the people of Israel like a hot wind punishes the desert vegetation, the punishment still was not as great as that of Israel's enemies.

When all of Israel's sins have been expiated, there will be no more idol worship in the land. The *Asherim* are Semitic cult goddesses represented by standing wooden objects. Neither they nor the incense altars they stand on will remain in the land.

Verse 10 mentions a city that will be deserted. Perhaps the city is Jerusalem; the text does not identify it. The description of the city sounds like the lonely city of Lamentations 1:1. The animals can graze in the heart of the city, for it has now turned into pastureland. Women follow the sheep and cattle around, gathering sticks for firewood. The people have no discernment; they cannot distinguish between good and evil.

Concluding Oracle (27:12-13)

This oracle brings Chapter 27 to a conclusion with a message of triumph. The message is delivered in two parts, each introduced with the formula *in that day*. First, at the end of time there will be a harvest across the whole area from Egypt to Mesopotamia. At that harvest, God will distinguish between the chaff (to be judged) and the grain (to be gathered and brought to Israel).

Secondly, *in that day* a trumpet will sound to announce to those exiled in Assyria and Egypt that it is time to return to Jerusalem. The image of the returned exiles worshiping together *on the holy mountain of Jerusalem* is an appropriate conclusion to the apocalypse as a whole.

§ § § § § § §

The Message of Isaiah 24–27

Within the Book of Isaiah, these chapters stand apart from the rest of the book. What message do they convey about God and about humankind?

§ No matter how desperate the situation, there is always room for hope in the future of a restored Jerusalem.

§ The people must rely on their trust in God to help them through times of despair.

§ One day in the future, God will judge the rulers of Israel's enemies. They will have to pay for their actions.

§ We cannot always predict or understand what miracles God will perform on our behalf.

§ Trust in God will provide for the people strength they did not know they had.

§ Human beings can only accomplish so much. After that they must trust that God's power will work effectively.

§ § § § § § §

Isaiah 28–30

Introduction to These Chapters

Most of Chapters 28–35 consists of oracles concerning Judah (the Southern Kingdom), and Israel (the Northern Kingdom, here called Ephraim). Chapters 28–30 contain an oracle about Samaria's religious leaders, an oracle about the political leaders in Jerusalem, a parable, an oracle about the future restoration of Judah, and a group of oracles about hypocrisy in the religious practices of the people.

Here is an outline of Chapters 28–30.

    I. Oracles Against Religious Leaders (28:1-13)
       A. Oracle concerning Ephraim (28:1-4)
       B. God's future blessing (28:5-6)
       C. Oracle concerning Judah (28:7-13)
   II. Oracles Against Political Leaders (28:14-22)
  III. Parable of the Farmer (28:23-29)
  IV. Restoration of Judah (29:1-8)
   V. Miscellaneous Oracles (29:9-24)
  VI. Oracles Concerning Egypt (30:1-17)
       A. Ambassadors sent to Egypt (30:1-7)
       B. Judah's alliance with Egypt (30:8-17)
 VII. Restoration of Judah (30:18-26)
VIII. Oracle Against Assyria (30:27-33)

Oracle Concerning Ephraim (28:1-4)

This oracle concerns Ephraim (Israel) and its capital city, Samaria. Its message concerns the future destruction of the city by the Assyrian army in 722 B.C. The specific woe is addressed to the rulers in the city, who are drunkards and wear crowns on their heads. The *fading flower of its glorious beauty* is an allusion to the once-glorious city, now fading in its brilliance. Since they are *overcome with wine*, the rulers in the city are confused and do not understand what is happening to them.

Into this setting comes God, like a hailstorm bringing torrents of rain. As a result the rulers' crowns will be trampled in the mud. Verse 4 describes the results of the storm in detail. The *first ripe figs* are eaten right away, just as Samaria will be consumed by the Assyrians.

God's Future Blessing (28:5-6)

These two verses are a separate section introduced by the words *in that day*. The contrast here is to what will happen to Samaria (in verses 1-4). The *crown of Ephraim* will be trodden in the mud, but God will be a *crown of glory* for the remnant of the people. God will protect the people by bringing a *spirit of justice* to the leaders in the city, and by turning back any attacks by outsiders.

Oracle Concerning Judah (28:7-13)

These verses pick up the theme of verses 1-4, but direct the address to Judah rather than Samaria. Judah's leaders also are guilty of drunkeness, especially the priests and the prophets. Presumably, these priests and prophets were opponents of Isaiah, who happened to witness the scene he describes, in all its ugly details. Leviticus 10:9-10 specifies that priests are not to drink wine or strong drink. These priests obviously were violating cultic law. Their behavior has caused a blurring of their vision and their judgment. Verses 9 and 10 speak of the prophet's frustration. No one will listen to him. Verse 10 imitates the prophet's words in a mocking way.

Verses 11-13 allude to the Assyrians, who speak a language different from those dwelling in Judah. God will speak to the people through the Assyrians rather than using the mouth of Isaiah, since no one will listen to him.

Verse 12 summarizes the message of Isaiah, which will now be given to the people in another way. Verse 13 repeats the words of verse 10, for the purpose of added emphasis. Surely the people will now understand.

Oracles Against Political Leaders (28:14-22)

This rather lengthy section is divided into two parts: an accusation of the scoffers (verses 14-15) and a warning to the unfaithful (verses 16-22).

Therefore, at the beginning of verse 14, links this message with what precedes it (the people have not heeded earlier warnings). This warning is addressed to a group of *scoffers, who rule this people in Jerusalem.* In making an arrangement with the underworld they are behaving as though they are immune from the power of death. Perhaps the prophet is alluding to the tendency to ignore the Assyrian threat, or to act as if the threat can be turned back solely by human hands. The rulers must count on God for help, not solely on other human beings. The end of verse 15 states the folly of that approach.

Verse 16 describes God's laying of the enigmatic *cornerstone* in Zion/Jerusalem. Commentators have suggested many interpretations of the cornerstone: God's law, God's Temple, the Davidic monarchy, and so forth. Whatever its exact meaning is, we can be certain that it symbolizes salvation for the faithful. *He who believes will not be in haste* (another translation is *will not be moved.*)

The line and the plummet (verse 17) are instruments used in construction of new buildings or reconstruction of old structures. Justice and righteousness will be the standards God will use in dealing with Jerusalem in the future. The pact that the leaders had formerly made with the underworld will be of no use to them now. All will be destroyed by the storm of God's wrath. The people will not be able to cover themselves to avoid it.

Verse 21 mentions two former deeds of God that prove that God will act again in the future. The battle on Mount

Perazim was a defeat of the Philistines (see 2 Samuel 5:17-21). In the conquest in the valley of Gibeon, a group of Canaanite kings were defeated by the Israelites due to a miraculous intervention by God (see Joshua 10:9-28).

Verse 22 gives one last warning directed to the scoffers: do not scoff or you will be worse off than you are already. God has decreed destruction.

Parable of the Farmer (28:23-29)

The parable is introduced by a call to attention in verse 23. Verse 24 contains a rhetorical question, to which the anticipated answer is *no*. Of course, a farmer does not plow all the time, without thought of when and where the plowing should take place. The extended question in verse 25 expects the answer *yes*. Of course, the farmer sows the proper seeds in the proper places. Verse 26 summarizes the situation: The farmer knows when and where to plant which kinds of seeds. He does everything according to a logical plan.

Verses 27-29 make a similar point by explaining some of the earlier references in the parable. Dill and cummin, spices used in cooking, are too soft to be threshed with a sledge. The proper tools must be used—a rod and a stick. The farmer must also know just how long the threshing should last (verse 28). Acting according to a logical plan and using the proper tools are both necessary in successful farming. According to verse 29, God acts in the same way in dealing with the people of Judah.

Restoration of Judah (29:1-8)

This oracle is divided into three parts: verses 1-3, verses 4-6, and verses 7-8. As a whole, the oracle moves from a warning about future judgment into a prophecy of salvation. We can see the transition in the middle of verse 5, with the words *and in an instant, suddenly* . . . .

Verse 1 begins with an address to *Ariel,* another name for Jerusalem. Many suggestions have been made for an exact translation of this word, including mountain of God, lion of God, hero, fire pit, and altar hearth. We do know that the word symbolizes the city of Jerusalem. *Like an Ariel* (in verse 2) means either *like an inhabitant of the underworld* or *like a burning. The city where David encamped* refers to the fact that David once dwelled in Jerusalem and made the city his capital.

The people living in Jerusalem are celebrating their feasts year after year, completely unaware of what is soon to befall them. The prophet knows, however. An enemy army is about to surround the city and attack its gates. Just at the time the attack takes place, a voice of God will sound from deep in the earth.

Verses 4-6 describe a transition from doom to deliverance. At the moment when Jerusalem is in greatest distress, the city will beg God to rescue it. The image is of a dying person who has fallen down and who cries to God from the dust. God will respond by a visitation accompanied by thunder, earthquake, wind, and fire (traditional accompaniments of God's presence). As a result of this visitation, Jerusalem's enemies will be turned back.

Verses 7-8 state that the attack on Jerusalem described in verses 2-3 will seem like it was only a dream. Just as a hungry man dreams only of being filled up, the enemies of Jerusalem will wake up to discover that their conquest of the city came to nothing.

Miscellaneous Oracles (29:9-24)

Verses 9-12 form the first portion of this larger section. These verses continue the theme prominent in Chapter 28—warning against drunkenness and the resulting confusion about God's purposes. The prophet seems to be saying to Jerusalem's leaders, "Go ahead, continue on your way. But just know that in the future you will see the folly of your ways." The prophet describes the leaders' insensitivity in various ways. They are drunk; they are blinded. They are in a deep sleep. They cannot read what has been written for them, especially since they cannot even open the book.

Verses 13-14 warn against false piety. The people are accused of worshiping God only with their lips, not with their hearts. In the future, the people will have a new attitude toward God and worship. False *wisdom* and *discernment* will be replaced by a true attitude of worship.

Verses 15 and 16 are a cry of woe uttered against those who have made political decisions without consulting God. These people are operating backwards. In the same way that the clay is subject to the potter, the leaders in Jerusalem should be subject to God. The prophet is probably referring here to the proposed alliance with Egypt against Assyria, around 701 B.C.

Verses 17-24 are a prophecy of future salvation. It is addressed to the meek and the poor, who have been oppressed by ruthless people. Verse 17 opens with a question: Will it not be soon that our land will be fruitful again? The implied answer is *Yes, it will happen soon*. The deaf, blind, meek, and poor—the outcasts of society—will be exalted in that day. *The Holy One of Israel* is a name for God found in many places in Isaiah's prophecies.

Verses 20-21 promise that when salvation comes society will be just. There will be no more ruthless people in the courts. Laws and execution of laws will be fair; there will be no discrimination against any element of society.

Verse 22 identifies God as the same God who redeemed Israel many years ago. When the people realize what God has done for them, they will repent and return to a right relationship with God.

Ambassadors Sent to Egypt (30:1-7)

About the time the Assyrians began threatening the city of Jerusalem (during Hezekiah's reign, at the end of the eighth century), Hezekiah sent a group of ambassadors to Pharaoh Shabako, in Egypt. Hezekiah's plan was to enlist the aid of Egyptian forces in defense against Assyria. This decision was made without consulting God and against the advice of Isaiah, as is made clear in verses 1-3. The results are clear. The plan will fail, and the people of Judah will be reduced to humiliation.

Verses 6-7 describe the journey of these ambassadors from Jerusalem through the Negeb (desert) to Egypt. Traveling through an unknown land will bring many dangers, and all this will come to nought anyway. The people of Egypt *cannot profit them.* Verse 7 gives the final judgment. Rahab, a mythological sea dragon, will sit still.

Judah's Alliance With Egypt (30:8-17)

Verse 8 introduces this section with instructions to the prophet to write his words in a book, to preserve them for posterity. Verses 9-11 give the reason for this instruction. The nation of Israel has rejected Isaiah's message, and so has been disobedient to God. The people prefer to hear *smooth things* (that which is easy to hear) rather than what is right.

Verses 12-14 describe the results of the people's actions. If they are not interested in what is right, God will judge them. Punishment will come when they least expect it.

Verses 15-17 portray the people's response. God gives the choice clearly in verse 15. Return to me, and you will be saved. The people's refusal is described in terms of their trust in military strength. But God repeats that such surface solutions will not work in the end.

Restoration of Judah (30:18-26)

Verse 18 proclaims the assurance that salvation is near. God is just, and ready to show mercy to the people.

Verses 19-26 describe the coming of salvation in greater detail. The inhabitants of Jerusalem will no longer weep. If they call to God, God will hear them and respond. Verse 20 mentions a teacher, which should probably be read as a plural, *teachers* or *prophets.* Bread and water will fulfill all the people's needs. They will not deviate from the way of God, to the right or the left.

According to verse 22, idolatry will come to a end in the restored nation. The land will become fertile again (verses 23-25). Rain will fall and grain will grow in abundance. The sun and moon will be brighter, so there will be no distinction between night and day.

Oracle Against Assyria (30:27-33)

Here prophecies concerning Assyria are interwoven with a song of deliverance. God comes from far away with smoke, fire, and water. God's wrath is like a torrent of water that covers a man up to his neck.

When God comes in this manner the people of Judah will be glad (verses 29-30). They are not to be punished. Rather, *the Assyrians will be terror-stricken.*

Verse 33 mentions *a burning place,* otherwise known as Topheth, a valley to the south of Jerusalem where sacrifices were made. *The King* is known as Molech, an Ammonite deity to whom children were sacrificed.

§ § § § § § §

The Message of Isaiah 28–30

§ The restored world in the future is the same world that exists now. It is the people who will be changed.

§ In the face of danger, appealing to military might will do no good. The people must rely on God.

§ Obedience to God requires trust in God.

§ We may not always understand God's purposes.

§ Hope helps us endure the trials of this world.

§ Asking what is God's will is the best way to make plans, no matter what the task.

§ When the people see what God can do, they will have no choice but to behave.

§ § § § § § §

Isaiah 31–33

Introduction to These Chapters

Chapters 31–33 continue the series of oracles concerning Egypt that began in Chapter 28. This present section includes oracles concering Egypt, Assyria, the women of Judah, and the future age of justice, as well as a section describing the coming of the Spirit, and a prophetic liturgy (in Chapter 33).

Here is an outline of Chapters 31–33.
 I. Oracles Concerning Egypt and Others (31:1–32:20)
   A. Oracle against Egypt (31:1-3)
   B. Oracles against Sennacherib (31:4-9)
   C. The future of Judah (32:1-8)
   D. Oracle against Judah's women (32:9-14)
   E. Outpouring of the Spirit (32:15-20)
 II. Prophetic Liturgy (33:1-24)
   A. Part one (33:1-6)
   B. Part two (33:7-16)
   C. Part three (33:17-24)

Oracle Against Egypt (31:1-3)

As in several of his earlier prophecies, Isaiah speaks out against Hezekiah's request for aid from Egypt against the Assyrian threat. Hezekiah and his advisors relied solely on military might and not at all on God, who is the ultimate protector. Not only that, they did not even consult God in their plans. Because they have done this, God will punish them further (verse 2). Verse 3 is reminiscent of the crossing of the Israelites at the Red Sea (see Exodus 13–14). The prophet wants his audience to understand the difference between the kind of help the Egyptians can give and what God can do.

Oracle Against Sennacherib (31:4-9)

Here the prophet speaks words that God has put into his mouth. Just as a lion is not afraid of a band of shepherds, God will not be deterred by the Assyrian threat. God will protect Jerusalem just as birds tend to hover over nests that hold their young.

Verses 6 and 7 are, according to most commentators, a later addition. They contain an admonition to the people to return to God, and to cast away their false idols.

Verse 8 continues the oracle against Sennacherib of Assyria. *Assyria shall fall by a sword, not of man*; the implication is that God's sword will be responsible for Assyria's downfall. *His rock* (verse 9) is a reference to the Assyrian king, who will die as the army flees in terror. The *fire* and *furnace* are the altar in the Temple in Jerusalem, the dwelling place of God.

The Future of Judah (32:1-8)

This oracle describes what the coming age will be like for Judah's society. It is divided into two parts: verses 1-5 and verses 6-8. In verses 1-5 the prophet describes a just society; in verses 6-8 the prophet discusses the differences between noble men and fools.

The opening two verses speak of a king and his princes who will rule in justice and righteousness. Their reign of justice will be like a protective cover from the wind and rain, and will feel like a stream of water feels to a patch of dry earth. This kind of society is in sharp contrast to the way things are now, and will be in the near future. *The eyes of those who see* are the eyes of court officials. They will not be closed to justice. In contrast to those now guilty of making rash and harsh judgments, those who judge in the future will do so with cool rationality.

Verses 5-8 discuss the differences between nobles and fools. For in the age to come, people will be able to distinguish clearly between these two groups. At the present time, nobles are called fools and fools are called nobles. Fools *practice ungodliness*; they are not obedient to the will of God. That causes them to ignore the needs of their neighbors as well. Noble persons, on the other hand, plan and carry out deeds of righteousness.

Oracle Against Judah's Women (32:9-14)

This oracle is addressed to a group of Judean women who are *at ease*, or complacent in their attitude. The prophet says that things may be going well now, but within *a little more than a year* circumstances will change drastically. Why? Because the grape and fruit harvest will fail. Although we are not told why there will be no harvest, we can assume that the land will be devastated so that no crops will be able to grow.

Verse 11 mentions sackcloth, a garment worn while in mourning. These women are being told to mourn for the fate of Judah. This command is continued and made more specific in verses 12-14.

Outpouring of the Spirit (32:15-20)

The word *until*, which begins this oracle, ties it closely with the preceding address to the women of Judah. In fact, these verses bring resolution to the atmosphere of anxiety created in verses 9-14. When the Spirit is poured out, history will be transformed. God's Spirit represents God's power, which cannot be matched. This oracle must have been pleasing to an audience that was aware of what was to come before the dawn of salvation. Israel will dwell in peace and security, in justice and righteousness. *And the forest will utterly go down* might also be translated *and it will hail when the forest comes down*, a reference to the former destruction of the city. Verse 20 brings the oracle to a confident conclusion.

Prophetic Liturgy, Part One (33:1-6)

Verse 1 introduces the liturgy as a whole, with the formula *Woe . . . .* The following verses speak of an attack on the city of Jerusalem, followed by a defeat of the enemy and the restoration of the city. The whole section is called a prophetic liturgy because it was evidently intended to be spoken aloud in a service of worship.

The woe is addressed to a *destroyer*, an unnamed tyrant who has yet to be destroyed. Destruction is predicted for this tyrant at some time in the future.

Verse 2 contains a congregational prayer. *Be our arm* is a request that God give strength to the people. They have no army they can depend on. Verses 3-6 describe God's response to their request. In verse 5, God promises to restore Jerusalem to its former glory. Justice and righteousness will prevail; the people will fear (obey) God.

Part Two (33:7-16)

Verses 7-9 continue the words of the congregation, but here the form is that of a lament. The people weep over what will happen when the tyrant comes. The land will no longer be a place where persons can sojourn. The fields will become infertile. No one can make treaties or negotiate for peace. Lebanon, Sharon, Bashan, and Carmel will all be barren; in other words, the whole area will not produce.

In verse 10, God decides it is time to intervene. God speaks directly to Israel's enemies, promising to destroy them completely. They will be forced to admit the power of God (verse 13).

At first, the inhabitants of Jerusalem see what God is doing and they are afraid. God's acts of destruction will affect them, too. Verse 15 describes those persons who will survive the devastation: those who are righteous and just, guiltless and peaceloving. The needs of those persons will be provided for.

Part Three (33:17-24)

These verses describe the king, or ruler, at the time
when salvation comes to Israel. First, however, it will be
necessary for the people to look back on the terrors of the
past (verses 17-19). Looking back on the past will help
the people understand the immense contrast between
what has been and what will be. What will be is
described in verses 20-24.

Jerusalem will be quiet and peaceful, not the habitation
of wars and destruction. The people will never again
have to move; they will dwell securely. There will be
enough water to supply the needs of the city. Verse 22
affirms what has been said with a song of praise to the
God who will bring it all about.

Verses 23 and 24 describe what will happen to ships
that sail near Jerusalem (presumably up the Jordan River).
They will suddenly be unable to steer or sail on a straight
course. Then, even the lame would be able to come
aboard and plunder their treasures.

§ § § § § § §

The Message of Isaiah 31–33

§ Humankind can hope for peace, if persons will repent
and return to God.

§ God is capable of actions that seem to be impossible.

§ Our actions should be directed first to God and then
on behalf of one another.

§ In the glorious future that God promised to bring
about, the prophet believed that society would be
different from the way it was in his day.

§ Those who can remember days of darkness and
despair are better able to look towards a bright future.

§ § § § § § §

Isaiah 34–35

Introduction to These Chapters

These two short chapters form a conclusion to the series of oracles in Isaiah 28–33, in the same way that Chapters 24–27 conclude Chapters 13–23. The material in this section concerns the fate of the enemies of Judah and the final restoration of Jerusalem.

Because much of the language and imagery in these two chapters is similar to that of Chapters 40–55, the work of Second Isaiah, many commentators consider these chapters to have been originally part of Second Isaiah's prophecies. We have no way of knowing for certain.

Here is an outline of Chapters 34–35.

I. Judgment on God's Enemies (34:1-17)
   A. God will judge the world (34:1-4)
   B. God will punish Edom (34:5-17)
II. Restoration of Zion (35:1-10)

God Will Judge the World (34:1-4)

This section is introduced by a call to attention—a series of imperatives addressed to the nations, the peoples, the earth, and the world. The message begins in verse 2. God is angry at the nations and has handed them over to be slaughtered.

As verse 4 indicates, the nations will come to an inglorious end. *The host of heaven* (stars and constellations) will come loose and fall to the ground like leaves fall off a tree in the autumn season.

God Will Punish Edom (34:5-17)

A similar oracle of judgment upon Edom is found in Jeremiah 49:7-22. Edom here represents all of Israel's enemies, but is also singled out for special treatment. Out of the skies, which are dark because the stars have fallen to the ground, the sword of God falls down upon Edom. The sword is covered with the blood of animals that are usually used for sacrificial rituals. *Bozrah* is mentioned in verse 6; it was a prominent Edomite city located southeast of the Dead Sea.

Verse 8 gives the reason for the destruction of Edom: God desires vengeance on Edom for its treatment of Judah. Amos 1:11-12 describes what Edom has done to Judah in the past. Edom pursued its brother (Judah) with the sword, and was without mercy.

Verses 9-15 describe the results of God's vengeance on Edom. The prophet considered the fate of Edom similar to that of Sodom and Gomorrah (see Genesis 19), presumably because the sin of Edom was as great as that of those two cities. Edom will burn night and day, forever.

Verse 11 describes the total desolation of the country. Wild birds will live in the land; it will be as the primeval chaos. Its name will be *No Kingdom There*, indicating what will ultimately happen. Verses 13-15 continue the graphic description of what Edom will be like after its destruction. The *night hag* (verse 14) describes Lilith, an ancient Mesopotamian storm demon.

Verses 16-17 imagine a future day when the Scripture will be read through, and all the events foretold there will have come to pass.

Restoration of Zion (35:1-10)

These verses describe the restored land of Judah as fertile and lush, in comparison to the desolate land of Edom described in the previous chapter. Verses 1-6 describe what will happen when God returns to the land.

The wilderness and the desert are common images in Second Isaiah as well. The final phrase in verse 2 states that *they shall see the glory of the Lord*. Who *they* are is uncertain. Perhaps verse 3 makes the reference clear.

In verses 3 and 4, the people who are now weak and feeble will be strengthened by virtue of God's coming. The image is of weakened prisoners, on their hands and knees, waiting for God.

Verse 5 states that the eyes and ears of the blind and deaf will be opened. The prophet could be referring to either physical or spiritual impairments, or both. Verse 6 continues the reference to physical impairments, perhaps again with symbolic references. According to the second part of verse 6, the deserts will no longer be dry when God arrives at the time of salvation.

Verse 8 mentions a highway, called the *Holy Way*, that will pass through the desert. No one who is unclean will walk on this highway, for it is God's highway. This image matches the *highway of our God* mentioned in 40:3. Animals will not walk along this highway and threaten the safety of its travelers. Rather, those ransomed will return to Judah along this road. They will walk along the road singing songs of joy and praise to God.

§ § § § § § §

The Message of Isaiah 34–35

§ Failure to get along with its neighbors caused Judah to look to God for help and protection.

§ God will have revenge on those nations who deal unjustly with God's people.

§ God will come to save those who believe, even though they may have suffered in the past.

§ § § § § § §

Isaiah 36–39

Introduction to These Chapters

Chapters 36–39 are the only lengthy narrative section in the Book of Isaiah. Much of the material found in these chapters is found also in 2 Kings 18–20. Most commentators think that the narrative in 2 Kings was written first, and portions of it were used in Isaiah 36–39.

Chapter 39 contains a number of references to the Exile into Babylon, and so is a transitional chapter in the book as a whole (Chapters 40–50 come from the time of the Babylonian Exile).

Here is an outline of Isaiah 36–39.

I. Attack on Jerusalem (36:1-22)
   A. Do not rely on Egypt (36:1-12)
   B. Rabshakeh's speech to Jerusalem (36:13-20)
   C. The people's response (36:21-22)

II. Isaiah Advises Hezekiah (37:1-38)
   A. Hezekiah goes to the Temple (37:1-7)
   B. Hezekiah is challenged again (37:8-20)
   C. Isaiah responds (37:21-29)
   D. Hezekiah is reassured (37:30-35)
   E. The Assyrians are defeated (37:36-38)

III. Hezekiah's Illness (38:1-22)
   A. God responds with a sign (38:1-8)
   B. Hezekiah's song (38:9-20)
   C. Concluding verses (38:21-22)

IV. Merodach-baladan and Hezekiah (39:1-8)

Do Not Rely on Egypt (36:1-12)

This section begins a longer section, which concludes at the end of Chapter 37, and which gives us historical background from the year 701 B.C.. Sennacherib, king of Assyria, was threatening to destroy the city of Jerusalem. King Hezekiah (king in Judah at the time) was being advised by the prophet Isaiah on how to handle the Assyrian threat. Isaiah's advice was essentially, Don't rely on Egypt. Sennacherib will be defeated anyway. These verses are duplicated in 2 Kings 18:13-27.

Verse 1 dates this section precisely, *in the fourteenth year of King Hezekiah*, or 701 B.C.. According to historical records from the Babylonian kings, Jerusalem had forty-six fortified cities at the time of Sennacherib's attack. If he conquered all those cities, King Hezekiah had good reason to be worried.

The Rabshakeh, sent by Sennacherib to warn Hezekiah of impending defeat, was a high-ranking officer in Sennacherib's court. The name was actually a title, not the man's proper name. This man *stood by the conduit of the upper pool in Jerusalem*, in the same place King Ahaz was confronted by the prophet Isaiah thirty years earlier (see Isaiah 7:1-9). Hezekiah evidently sent three of his own court officials out to meet the Rabshakeh: Eliakim, Shebna, and Joash. Eliakim and Shebna have been mentioned previously in an oracle of warning against their activities (see Isaiah 22).

The Rabshakeh's purpose in this encounter is to frighten Hezekiah and his officials. He argues that it would be useless to resist any further; the might of the Assyrian army is too great. There is no use relying on Egypt for help, since that country is *a broken reed of a staff* that will turn against anyone who makes an alliance with it. Isaiah preached the same message in 31:1-3.

Likewise do not, says the Rabshakeh, delude yourselves into thinking that your God can save you. This statement (verse 7) repeats the description of

Hezekiah's reform found in 2 Kings 18:4, and indicates a basic misunderstanding of Hezekiah's purpose. In the theology of the Assyrians, one god could have many manifestations. The Assyrians assumed that Hezekiah was removing elements of Yahweh (the God of Israel) worship, when he was actually destroying all manifestations of other gods.

In verses 8-10, the Rabshakeh presents Hezekiah's officers with a challenge. The Assyrians will give them 2,000 horses if they can find enough riders in the army of the Israelites. Unfortunately, the Israelite army is not that numerous. The message is that even horses and chariots cannot help them now. In verse 10, the Assyrian is arrogant enough to claim that what he intends to do to Jerusalem he is doing in the name of Israel's God.

According to verse 11, Hezekiah's officers request that the Rabshakeh speak to them in the Aramaic language, which was the official language used in diplomatic negotiations. According to the Hebrew officials, Aramaic should be used rather than Hebrew because the people standing close by (on top of the city wall) did not need to understand what was being said. Since the common people did not understand Aramaic, using that language would solve the problem. However, their plan backfires, because this request gives the Rabshakeh the idea of addressing his speech not just to the officials, but to everyone. The end of verse 12 gives the graphic details of what will happen to the people of Jerusalem as a result of the Assyrian siege.

Rabshakeh's Speech to Jerusalem (36:13-20)

In delivering this speech to the whole population of Jerusalem, the Assyrian is hoping their anxiety will spread to the king and his leaders, encouraging their decision to surrender. The main point of the message is: Give up, because not Hezekiah, not even your God, can save you now. Sennacherib, through his emissary, advises the people to surrender now, and he promises to treat them well. (The implication is that if they fight back against the Assyrians, their fate will be not nearly so promising.)

Verse 19 mentions the city of Samaria, capital of the Northern Kingdom. That should remind the people that their God would not necessarily come to their aid, since that city was destroyed twenty years earlier. (For the locations of other cities mentioned in verse 19, see the Glossary and maps.)

The People's Response (36:21-22)

According to verse 21, the people did not answer the Rabshakeh, because the king had ordered them not to. The three officials now return to the king to report the message. They had rent their clothes, symbolizing the urgency of the situation and the potential for disaster implicit in the Rabshakeh's words.

Hezekiah Goes to the Temple (37:1-7)

Hezekiah also tears his garments when he hears the news, and goes to the Temple, which is in the heart of the city. He sends his officials to consult with Isaiah. In Israel's history, the relationships between kings and prophets was often close, so that kings consulting prophets in times of crisis was a common occurrence. David, Israel's first great king, had a close relationship with the prophet Nathan. (See especially 2 Samuel 7.)

The message King Hezekiah sends Isaiah is of extreme urgency. Verses 1-6 use the image of a woman who is about to give birth but is unable to. Such a woman needs help immediately. They ask Isaiah for a prayer on behalf of the people of Jerusalem.

In verses 5-7 the prophet Isaiah replies to the king's messengers, and his answer must have given comfort to the king. Isaiah speaks on God's behalf, saying that God will cause Sennacherib to return home after hearing rumors of domestic unrest. When Sennacherib returns to Assyria, he will die.

Hezekiah Is Challenged Again (37:8-20)

This section describes a second challenge by Sennacherib of King Hezekiah. This event probably took place toward the end of Isaiah's ministry (687 B.C.). King Sennacherib is waging war on the city of Libnah, a town just north of Lachish, in the southern hill country of Judah. He has heard a rumor that King Tirhakah of Ethiopia has set out against him. Sennacherib again sends messengers to Hezekiah, warning him of imminent defeat by the Assyrian army. Sennacherib mentions Gozen, Haran, Rezeph, and Eden to remind Hezekiah that these cities are located in Mesopotamia. The cities mentioned in verse 13 also met a similar end.

Verses 14-20 narrate Hezekiah's reaction to this second challenge. The letter given to him was probably written on a scroll. Hezekiah's first response is to go immediately to the Temple to speak to God. His prayer is introduced with liturgical language that describes God's majesty. The prayer's main theme is that God alone can save the people of Judah, despite what Sennacherib claims. In effect, King Hezekiah is asking God to prove Sennacherib wrong.

Isaiah Responds (37:21-29)

Isaiah here gives the answer of God to Hezekiah's prayer, introduced by the first few words in verse 22. God's words will have to do with Sennacherib (*concerning him*, verse 22). In fact, the speech is addressed directly to Assyria's king. *She* (in verse 22) refers to the city of Jerusalem. Isaiah's response comes to Sennacherib in the form of a taunt song. Wagging the head signifies a mocking attitude.

The message of the song is that Sennacherib will be punished for mocking the God of Israel. Not only that, he has plundered the valuable forests of Lebanon. God, however, has the power to determine the course of history, including the actions of Assyria. The irony is that while Sennacherib thought he was performing brilliant military maneuvers of his own volition, Israel's God was guiding him all the time. For his arrogance Sennacherib will be severely punished; verse 29 describes his fate vividly.

Hezekiah Is Reassured (37:30-35)

In verse 30 the addressee changes from Sennacherib to Hezekiah. The message from God is that in the third year from now, the situation in Judah will return to normal. The harvest that will be reaped in that year symbolizes the growth in population that will also occur. All this will take place at the hand of God.

In addition, Sennacherib will not be allowed to ever enter into the city of Jerusalem, much less to attack the city. *For the sake of my servant David* reminds Hezekiah of God's original promise that the descendants of David would prosper in Jerusalem (see 2 Samuel 17).

The Assyrians Are Defeated (37:36-38)

The disaster described in these verses fulfills the promise made by God in the previous verses. *The angel of the Lord* slew 185,000 Assyrians while they were asleep in their camp. This event is reminiscent of the slaying of all Egypt's first-born the night before the Exodus from Egypt (see Exodus 12:29).

Verses 37-38 describe the ultimate fate of Sennacherib. After returning to Nineveh, he is slain in the temple of his god, by two of his sons.

God Responds With a Sign (38:1-8)

These events are narrated also in 2 Kings 20.

Isaiah comes to Hezekiah when the king is on his deathbed, and advises the king to *set your house in order,* for death is imminent. In response, Hezekiah offers a prayer to God asking for God's blessing on him. As a result, God decides to act differently. Isaiah is told to deliver the message to Hezekiah that he will be healed and will live for fifteen more years. (2 Kings 20 specifies that this healing will take place within three days.) God adds that Jerusalem, with its king, will be delivered from the hand of the Assyrians.

In order to prove that these promises will be fulfilled, God provides a sign (verse 7). God will cause the shadow on the sundial to move backwards. In the 2 Kings account, a fuller description is provided for this sign and its meaning. Hezekiah is offered a choice. Does he want the shadow to move forward or backward? Hezekiah chooses that the shadow be moved backward, thinking that this would be the more difficult feat to accomplish. God's accomplishment of this sign was proof to Hezekiah that he would indeed recover from his illness.

Hezekiah's Song (38:9-20)

First reading of this section shows that its language is similar to that of many of the psalms. Its form is that of an individual thanksgiving psalm. In this kind of psalm, an individual looks back on former distress and offers thanksgiving to God for deliverance from those circumstances. This kind of song is appropriate for Hezekiah, since God had delivered him from imminent death. The word *writing* (verse 9) is the same word translated *Miktam* throughout the Psalms.

Hezekiah looks back on his former situation, realizing that death was a certainty for him. Like the cords on a tent are plucked up from the ground, and like a piece of cloth is removed from the loom when the threads are cut, his life was going to come to an end (verse 12). His pain was so great that he could not sleep (verse 15).

Verses 16-20 begin to speak of what God has done on Hezekiah's behalf to turn his situation around. Because

God had forgiven his sins (verse 17), he was saved. For that reason, he will continue to offer praise to God for the rest of his life.

Concluding Verses (38:21-22)
These verses refer to Hezekiah's illness, and so may originally have been located after verse 6. Apparently the prophet knew what to do for Hezekiah's symptoms, and he commands that those measures be carried out.

Merodach-baladan and Hezekiah (39:1-8)
This part of the historical section is repeated in 2 Kings 20:12-19. These events follow the recovery of Hezekiah from his illness. A group of emissaries is sent from Assyria to Jerusalem to congratulate King Hezekiah on being healed from his illness. They also bring the king gifts and letters on behalf of the Assyrian king. King Hezekiah responds to all this attention by proudly showing off all his treasures. When questioned by Isaiah, Hezekiah naively admits that he showed these men everything he had. According to verses 5-7, God is not pleased with Hezekiah's arrogance. Soon the time will come when Hezekiah will have nothing to show off.

§ § § § § § §

The Message of Isaiah 36–39

§ Human beings are dependent upon God in times of despair or physical illness.

§ Praise and thanksgiving are an appropriate response when one is renewed after a time of tragedy.

§ Arrogance on the part of human beings will be punished.

§ § § § § § §

Introduction to Isaiah 40–55

We know almost nothing about the prophet who wrote Chapters 40–55 in the Book of Isaiah. Because this prophet's words are included within the Old Testament book we call Isaiah, he has been given the name *Second Isaiah*, or *Deutero-Isaiah*. As we will see when we examine his prophecies, Second Isaiah stands in the tradition of the prophet Isaiah. Their messages are interrelated.

Whereas the prophet Isaiah lived and worked in Judah, Second Isaiah was a prophet of the Exile. Although the book never states this explicitly, Second Isaiah probably ministered to the people while they were in exile in Babylon. The book contains many references to Babylon and to circumstances that existed there (see Chapter 47, for example). In addition, the prophet speaks often of returning home to Judah. In fact, Second Isaiah's prophecies begin and end on that subject. (See 40:3-5 and 55:12-13).

The Babylonian Exile began with the fall of Jerusalem in 587 B.C. The inhabitants were captured and taken to Babylon, where they lived until King Cyrus of Persia defeated Babylon in 539 B.C. Second Isaiah's prophecies were directed to those exiles, and were delivered shortly before their return to Judah in 538 B.C.

Second Isaiah has two main parts: oracles about God's activity in history (Chapters 40–48), and prophecies about the future restoration of Judah (Chapters 49–55).

The message of Second Isaiah's prophecies fits the historical circumstances of prophet and people well. The people are in exile. Cyrus is about to appear on the scene and release them, after fifty years of bondage in Babylon. In this context, the prophet preaches a message of trust in God and hope for an imminent return to their homeland.

Isaiah 40

Introduction to This Chapter

Chapter 40 begins the work of the prophet of the Exile. The message of this chapter is the heart of the message of the next fifteen chapters, which makes Chapter 40 an appropriate introduction to the prophet's work.

Here is an outline of Chapter 40.

I. Call to Announce God's Coming (40:1-11)
   A. First cry (40:1-2)
   B. Second cry (40:3-5)
   C. The prophet's call (40:6-8)
   D. Third cry (40:9-11)

II. God the Creator (40:12-31)
   A. Concerning the nations (40:12-17)
   B. Concerning princes and rulers (40:18-24)
   C. Concerning the heavenly host (40:25-26)
   D. Concerning the exiles (40:27-31)

First Cry (40:1-2)

Because this section begins the words of another prophet, we might expect a superscription or introduction, like that found in Isaiah 1:1. It is typical of this prophet that he tells us nothing about his date or his circumstances. Instead, this prophet's words begin with the cry *Comfort, comfort my people*. This cry corresponds to the concluding cry of the book: *Depart, depart, go out thence* (52:11).

The repetition of the word *comfort* is characteristic of the language of this prophet. Repeating an imperative verb indicates the urgency of the prophet's message.

Similar repetitions occur in 51:9; 52:1, 11. *My people* and *your God* are phrases often used to describe the covenant between God and the chosen people (see Exodus 19, for example). *Your God* indicates that the prophet is speaking, but on God's behalf.

Verse 2 summarizes the message of this prophet. Israel's *warfare* (the Revised Standard Version suggests also *time of service*) is ended. In other words, the exile into Babylon is soon to come to an end. Israel's sin is forgiven by God. That the prophet speaks of these events in the past indicates his certainty of what he is proclaiming. In other words, he is so convinced of the imminent end of the Babylonian Exile, that he speaks of the event as though it had already happened. This belief is a highlight of this prophet's message.

The people have already received double the punishment they might have had. In other words, in the prophet's mind (and God's) the people have suffered more than enough. Now their suffering is about to end.

Second Cry (40:3-5)

This second cry is spoken by an unidentified person to an unidentified audience. This voice commands that it is now time to *prepare the way of the Lord* in the wilderness (desert). This verse and the two that follow it are quoted directly in Luke 3:4-6. However, in Luke and the other Gospels, the words *in the wilderness* are taken as an identification of the location of the voice, rather than the place where the highway was to be built. Somewhere in the tradition (between the formation of Old and New Testaments) the exact meaning of this cry altered slightly. However, its essential message remains the same: It is time for a highway to be built on which the exiles will make their journey home. *The way of the Lord* is an important concept in the prophecies of Second Isaiah (see 42:16; 43:16, 19; 48:17; 49:11; 51:10).

Verse 4 mentions valleys that will be lifted up and

mountains that will be leveled, symbolizing obstacles that might be put in the way of the returning exiles. *The glory of the Lord* will be revealed to everyone at the same time. The phrase *the mouth of the Lord has spoken* concludes this part of the chapter.

The Prophet's Call (40:6-8)

These verses correspond to the call of the prophet that appears in most prophetic books. As a matter of fact, the only information we have about Second Isaiah comes to us in these three verses. They are introduced by a second voice, who says *Cry!* Again, we are not told who is speaking. Here, however, we do know who is addressed by the voice—the prophet himself.

The second phrase in verse 6 tells us the prophet's answer to the cry: *What shall I cry?* It is addressed to the unknown speaker. Ordinarily when prophets are called they voice some initial objections to their call, usually related to their own incapabilities. Here, the prophet's objection relates to the message he is called to proclaim. It appears to be unnecessary and futile, since human life is transitory. However, verse 8 answers the prophet's objection. Yes, it is true that human life is fleeting. But the message is important nevertheless, because *the word of our God will stand forever*. This *word* is a reference to the promises God has made to the people in the past.

Most commentators agree that the last phrase in verse 7 is a gloss, or a comment by a later reader. Glosses such as this one indicate what persons throughout the Old Testament tradition thought was important enough to need to be commented on or explained.

Third Cry (40:9-11)

The addressee in this third cry is specified as *Zion, herald of good tidings*. Zion is commanded to go up on a high mountain to proclaim a message of deliverance. Again, the prophet has the attitude that the message to be proclaimed concerns an event that has already taken place. The return from the Exile is described in terms of what God will do to bring it about. God's *arm* symbolizes might or power, which will be used on the people's behalf. Verse 11 describes the other side of God. God is mighty, but tender and nurturing as well. From beginning to end, Second Isaiah's message presupposes that none of this would be happening if it were not for God.

God the Creator (40:12-31)

This section is composed of four parts. The first three begin with rhetorical questions, and prepare the way for the final section (verses 27-31), which makes clear the theme of the whole unit.

Concerning the Nations (40:12-17)

The first section begins with a series of rhetorical questions. The implied answer is, no one could possibly perform such feats, no one except God. Verse 12 uses the verbs *measure*, *mark off*, *enclose*, and *weigh*. These words all relate to the process of weighing something to determine its exact proportion. The *waters*, the *heavens*, and the *earth* signify the universe as a whole.

Verses 13-14 describe God as the source of all wisdom. These same ideas are expressed in such passages as Job 38 and Proverbs 8. Verses 15-17 contain a metaphor constructed to show how little influence the nations have on God or on worldly affairs. When a bucket is filled up with water, one more drop makes very little difference. Likewise, when scales are weighing a certain amount of something, the dust that might have been on them before the substance was placed there to be weighed makes little difference in the total weight that is calculated. The message of this section is that the affairs of the nations matter as little as a drop of water or a particle of dust, in comparison to the greatness of God. God's greatness cannot be measured.

Concerning Princes and Rulers (40:18-24)

In these verses the message is that nothing can be compared to God. Again the section opens with a rhetorical question: *To whom then will you liken God?* The answer is, of course, *no one*. Verses 19-20 make the point that idols certainly cannot be compared with God.

Verses 21-24 celebrate God as the creator and lord of history, a theme that runs throughout the whole of Second Isaiah's prophecies. Verse 21 uses an interesting literary technique. Four questions are posed, one right after another. In the original Hebrew, each of these questions is a little longer than the one that precedes. In contrast to the previous questions in this unit, however, these questions demand an answer.

The *circle of the earth* (verse 22) refers to the vault of heaven that encircles the world. According to Job 22:14, God walks on this circle. From that vantage point, and because of God's incomparability, human beings are so small that they seem like grasshoppers. In verses 23-24 the princes and rulers are singled out as amounting to nothing in the face of God's power and majesty.

Concerning the Heavenly Host (40:25-26)

The theme of God's incomparability is continued. Verse 26 alludes to the sun, moon, and stars when it says, *Lift up your eyes on high and see*. Then the question is raised, *who created these?* The answer is, of course, God. The irony in this verse is related to the fact that in Babylonia, where these prophecies originated, the sun, moon, and stars were gods to be worshiped. To say that Israel's God, Yahweh, created these elements, was a bold proclamation to make in this context.

Concerning the Exiles (40:27-31)

This final section makes clear the message of the whole unit (40:12-31): God will protect the people of Israel in their time of need. Verse 27 expresses the people's despair, perhaps using words that the prophet has heard directly from their mouths during services of worship. *My way is hid from the Lord, and my right is disregarded by my God.* In other words, God has forsaken me. This same sentiment is expressed often in the psalms, in individual lament songs.

The questions that open verse 28 are the same as those found in verse 21. The answer to the question—the message to the people in exile—is that the God who created the earth will remain with the people, even during times of despair. The strength and power God will give the people relates to the message of comfort that begins the book (40:1) and continues throughout the whole of Second Isaiah's prophecies.

§ § § § § § §

The Message of Isaiah 40

§ The exiled people were turning away from God, because they thought God had forsaken them. In the face of this attitude of despair, the prophet proclaims his message of comfort and hope.

§ The promise of deliverance the prophet brings is closely related to the fact that God has forgiven the sins of the people.

§ Just as God once delivered the Israelites from the hand of the Egyptians at the Red Sea, God will again prepare a way for the chosen people to escape their bondage and return home.

§ In response to what God is about to do for the people, they will renew their trust in God.

§ God is both creator and lord of history. Both these aspects of God are important to Second Isaiah's message.

§ § § § § § §

Isaiah 41–44

Introduction to These Chapters

These four chapters contain a series of speeches concerning the nations, the first of four servant songs, and a series of oracles concerning Judah's restoration. Here is an outline of these chapters.

I. Trial of the Nations (41:1-29)
   A. God stirs up Cyrus (41:1-5)
   B. The making of idols (41:6-7)
   C. Oracle of assurance (41:8-13)
   D. Oracle of assurance (41:14-16)
   E. God the creator (41:17-20)
   F. The Nations on Trial (41:21-29)
II. First Servant Song (42:1-4)
III. Oracle of Restoration (42:5-17)
   A. God is victorious (42:5-9)
   B. Call to praise (42:10-13)
   C. The lord of history (42:14-17)
IV. Israel's Judgment and Redemption (42:18–43:7)
   A. Concerning the blind and deaf (42:18-25)
   B. Redemption of Israel (43:1-7)
V. Israel's Restoration (43:8–44:8)
   A. The nations on trial (43:8-15)
   B. Proclamation of salvation (43:16-21)
   C. Israel on trial (43:22-28)
   D. Oracle of salvation (44:1-5)
   E. The nations on trial (44:6-8)
VI. Against Idolatry (44:9-20)
VII. Concluding Words (44:21-23)

God Stirs Up Cyrus (41:1-5)

These verses are a trial speech, in which God confronts the islands and nations in a courtroom setting. Other trial speeches in Second Isaiah are found in 41:21-29; 43:8-15; 44:6-8; and 45:20-25. In these trial speeches, the prophet is making the point that God is both creator and lord of history, and so is more powerful than all other gods. The gods of foreign nations and Israel's God both claim divinity. The prophet's point is that only one God can truly make this claim. The trial speeches prove this point again and again.

In verse 1, God speaks in the first person. God summons the coastlands (parts of the country that lie along the Mediterranean seacoast) to a trial. They are summoned to speak and be judged in the courtroom. Curiously, though, they are also summoned *in silence*. Perhaps they are to be silent as they enter the courtroom, and to speak only at the appropriate time.

Verses 2-4 describe God's *stirring up* of Cyrus, here identified as *one from the east. He gives us nations before him* refers to both God and Cyrus: He (God) causes Cyrus to be victorious over every nation he encounters. Verse 4 indicates the outcome of the trial. God is the only one powerful enough to use Cyrus as an instrument to bring about the restoration of the chosen people. God, who has been there from the beginning of time, will be there for the people until the end of time.

Verse 5 describes the verdict of the trial. The coastlands, who were summoned to trial in verse 1, now tremble in the presence of the all-powerful God of Israel.

The Making of Idols (41:6-7)

This short section is related to other parts of Second Isaiah that discuss the making of idols (40:19-20 and 44:9-20, for example). The people of Israel are forbidden by law to make graven images of God (see Exodus 20:4). Thus it was abhorrent to them to witness the kind of idol-making and idol worship that took place in Babylon. Second Isaiah intersperses harsh words about these practices throughout his prophecies.

Oracle of Assurance (41:8-13)

In this oracle the prophet assures his audience, the exiles, of future salvation at the hand of God. The oracle begins by turning attention to Israel, God's servant. Israel is described in a series of phrases lasting through the end of verse 9. The message of these phrases focuses on what God has done on Israel's behalf in the past. God has chosen, called, and established a friendship with Israel.

The message for Israel begins with verse 10. Israel is not to fear or be dismayed. The same God who accomplished marvellous things for Israel in the past will again come to the aid of the chosen people.

In verses 11-13, the nations are judged for what they have done to Israel. The last verse in this section gives the reason for the judgment against the nations. God is God, and there is no other God. The words *fear not* tie the beginning and end of this oracle together into one central message of comfort and salvation.

Oracle of Assurance (41:14-16)

In language and grammatical construction this oracle of assurance is quite similar to the one that precedes it (41:8-13). It begins with the words *fear not*, and is addressed to the people of Israel. Again, God is speaking to them in the first person.

The second half of verse 1 further identifies God as *redeemer* and *Holy One of Israel*, two designations found often in Second Isaiah's prophecies. *Holy One* is also used on many occasions in the earlier work of the prophet Isaiah (Chapters 1–39). Thus Second Isaiah can be seen as following in the tradition of his predecessor. The word *redeemer* comes from the Israelite legal system, where it refers to the next of kin, who is responsible for a widow after her husband (his brother) dies.

Verses 15-16 make the point that with God's help, the people can thresh the mountains and level the hills. As in the prologue in Chapter 40, mountains and hills represent obstacles in the way of the people's return to their homeland. When these obstacles are removed, the joyous return can take place.

God the Creator (41:17-20)

Verse 17 changes the subject entirely from what precedes in verses 14-16 (creation of a smooth road for the journey home). Here in verse 17 the subject is the poor and needy. When these persons want water, none is available. However, God's protection involves physical needs as well as spiritual comfort. God will provide water when the poor become thirsty.

The idea of water prompts the prophet to speak about the various places this water will come from. It will be found in rivers, fountains, pools, and springs. Then in verses 19-20, the people whose thirst will be quenched are symbolized by trees and other lush vegetation, which will grow freely in this newly-irrigated land. Verse 20 explains why all these things are taking place: so that persons will understand that God the creator is still working on their behalf.

The Nations on Trial (41:21-29)

As in the previous trial speech (see 41:1-5), God is bringing the nations to trial to settle the claims of divinity being made by their gods and the God of Israel. God speaks in the first person, summoning the nations to *set forth your case*. In other words, they are to lay out their argument before the court. The power that these gods of other nations have (or do not have) seems to depend on their ability to explain what they have accomplished in the past and what they intend to accomplish in the future.

Verse 24 is an important statement within the message of this prophet. Second Isaiah, living in Babylon with its many gods, proclaimed the superiority of Israel's God over all these lesser deities. The prophet does not categorically deny the existence of these other gods, but he comes close. Babylon's gods *are nothing;* their *work is nought.* But they still exist in that they can be summoned to court and judged wanting.

Verses 25-29 continue to judge the nations. *One from the north* refers to Cyrus, king of Persia, whose power was on the rise toward the end of the Babylonian Exile. *From the north* and *from the rising of the sun* (the east) combine to indicate the location of Persia, to the northeast of Babylonia and Israel as well.

To say that God *stirred up* Cyrus means that God used Cyrus as an instrument in the divine plan for the nation of Israel. This is not the first time God has used a foreign ruler in dealing with Israel. All through Chapters 1–39 in the Book of Isaiah, God is portrayed as using the nation of Assyria to punish the people of Israel. (See Isaiah 10:5, for example.) The main difference is that here in Second Isaiah, a foreign ruler is used by God to bring about the salvation of the chosen people, not judgment against them.

Verse 29 picks up the phraseology of verse 24.

First Servant Song (42:1-4)

This passage is the first of four servant songs found in Second Isaiah's prophecies. The other three songs are 49:1-6; 50:4-9; and 52:13–53:12. There are several very important things the prophet does not tell us in these songs: the identity of the servant, the nature of the task, and the circumstances of the servant's commissioning. The first issue is probably the most significant; commentators have written volumes discussing the identity of the servant. Is it Israel? Is it the prophet? Is it King Cyrus? Is it some other unknown person? We must realize that the servant's identity will remain hidden to us; perhaps that was the prophet's intention. What is most important is the message.

In verse 1 God is speaking about the servant, the one God chose and now upholds. God's commissioning of this servant is similar to the call of a prophet, except that the servant was apparently given his task in public. (God speaks to a group of people in verse 1, asking them to witness the event.)

Verses 1-4 tell us three things the servant will do: he will *bring forth justice to the nations,* he will *faithfully bring forth justice,* and he will *establish justice in the earth.* All these phrases are variations on the theme of bringing justice. According to verse 4, bringing justice means that God's law (teaching) will be known and obeyed by everyone.

Verse 4 could also be translated *He will not burn dimly or be bruised.* If this is the better translation, the allusion is to future suffering the servant will have to endure.

God Is Victorious (42:5-9)

This short section celebrates God as creator of the universe, who will also bring about the salvation of the chosen people. Throughout this section, God is speaking in the first person to an unknown individual.

The God who created heaven and earth is familiar language in Second Isaiah. God as creator is an intrinsic element of this prophet's theology. Verse 6 begins with the words, *I am the Lord.* This phrase, known as a *divine self-predication formula,* is common throughout Second Isaiah's prophecies. Its purpose is to single out God from among all the gods of foreign nations. God is the same God who first called the people into a covenant relationship.

This same God is now calling someone to come *as a covenant to the people.* God will use this person as an instrument of salvation. The reason for this activity is repeated in verses 8-9. God will be known as God above all other gods. Verse 9 brings the oracle to a conclusion by speaking of former things and new things—the continuity of God's actions in history.

Call to Praise (42:10-13)

This call to praise is the first of several that will be encountered in these chapters. (See also 44:23; 45:8; 48:20-21; 49:13; and 52:9-10.) All these calls to praise are structured in the same way. They begin with imperative verbs summoning someone or something to praise. They continue with phrases giving the reason(s) for praise, having to do with God's activity in history. They end with a promise of what God will do on behalf of the people in the future.

The initial summons in verse 10 echoes the opening words of Psalms 96 and 98. The people summoned to sing are then joined by the sea, the coastlands, the desert, the villages of Kedar, and the inhabitants of Sela. Kedar and Sela represent far-off nations; the meaning is that from the far corners of the earth people are being summoned to sing praises to God. We can imagine a mighty chorus celebrating the majesty of God.

Verse 13 gives the reason for this call to praise: God will be victorious over Israel's foes. The end result will be the return of the exiles to their homeland.

The Lord of History (42:14-17)

Verse 14 contrasts the God who was silent *for a long time* (for fifty years, during which the people were exiled) with the God who now cries out like a woman in labor. God will turn the fertile country into a barren wasteland (a contrast to 41:18, where the opposite is described). Here the fertile country is Babylon, which will be laid waste.

Verse 16 describes God leading the blind *in a way that they know not*, an allusion to the journey home from Babylon. The exiles were living in the darkness of despair that their God has forsaken them. But God answers, *I will not forsake them*. These words reinforce the message of comfort with which the book begins (40:1) and which is scattered throughout the words of this prophet.

Verse 17 describes the results of God's work. The Babylonian gods will be *utterly put to shame*.

Concerning the Blind and Deaf (42:18-25)

These words (and others like them) are the closest this prophet comes to judgment on the people of Israel. In general, the prophet felt that the people had suffered enough (40:1-2). That the people of Israel are deaf and blind means that they have been exiled so long they are almost immune to a message of hope and deliverance. Perhaps the people had complained that God would not hear their cries for help. In response, God says the people are the ones who are blind and deaf.

The words that Israel has used to describe its plight (verse 22) sound as though they could have been taken straight from a psalm. Perhaps these words were spoken aloud in public worship (see also 40:27).

Verses 23-25 remind the people of Israel that God has punished them for past sins. But now Israel must look to the future and the future saving acts that will be brought about by this same God.

Redemption of Israel (43:1-7)

These verses are the heart of Second Isaiah's message. They proclaim that God will comfort the people, and will lead them back to their homeland like a shepherd leads his flock. It begins with the words *But now*, which contrast this proclamation with the theme of judgment taken up in the preceding verses. This section is divided into two parts, each beginning with the command *Fear not* (verses 1 and 5).

In verse 1 God is called Israel's *redeemer*, or one who

has provided repayment for a debt. Verse 2 promises that on their way back home, God will protect the exiles when they *pass through the waters*. This promise alludes to the earlier presence of God with the Israelites at the crossing of the Red Sea. *Egypt* and *Ethiopia,* and *Seba* (Arabia) are all given to Israel as ransom. In other words, Cyrus will conquer these territories, working as God's instrument.

Verses 5-7 describe the journey home under God's guidance. God will gather the chosen people from afar, subduing all the nations that are holding them captive.

The Nations on Trial (43:8-15)

These verses are a trial speech similar to those found in 41:21-29 and 41:1-5. In verse 8 God commands the nations to produce witnesses. These witnesses are blind and deaf, although they have eyes and ears. God says the problem is with their attitude.

The verdict on the gods of the nations is that they cannot inspire confidence among their people that they are able to direct the course of history. God, on the other hand, has been proven to be the only God who is able to intervene in history. Verse 14 describes this intervention in detail: God will bring about Cyrus's defeat of Babylon.

Proclamation of Salvation (43:16-21)

This proclamation alludes to the miracle that took place at the Red Sea, and promises that a similar miracle is about to take place at the hand of God. Similar allusions to the Exodus can be found in 41:17-20 and 42:16. God advises the people to look to the future that lies ahead of them. Just as God provided water for the people during their wilderness wandering (see Exodus 17), God will again provide water to the returning exiles on their journey.

Israel on Trial (43:22-28)

Whereas in previous trial speeches God was calling the nations to account, here Israel is charged with ignoring

God. Israel's worship was not true worship. Verse 27 mentions Israel's *first father*, meaning Jacob. The prophet is probably referring to Jacob's stealing the birthright from his older brother Esau.

The *mediators* who sinned against God (verse 27) are unidentified in the passage, and this word is not found anywhere else in the Old Testament. Its meaning is uncertain.

Because of Israel's sins, God was forced to *deliver Jacob to utter destruction*. But that is not the final word, for the prophet's thought continues in 44:1.

Oracle of Salvation (44:1-5)

Yes, God delivered Israel to destruction. However, that statement made in 43:25 is followed directly with this salvation oracle. It begins with the words *But now hear* to show that there is a contrast to what precedes. *Who formed you from the womb* indicates that God created each person among the people of Israel.

Jeshurun (verse 2) is another name for Israel, of uncertain derivation. The term may come from the Hebrew word meaning *upright*.

The land is now *thirsty* and dry, signifying Judah's current situation. God intends to change that situation, causing vegetation to grow in abundance in the now-fertile soil. In addition to new vegetation, Israel as a nation will experience the turning of many persons of other faiths to God.

The Nations on Trial (44:6-8)

This short section is another trial speech of God against the nations (see also 41:1-5, 21-29; 43:8-15). The fact that the other nations cannot produce gods who can intervene in history on behalf of their people causes them to be judged wanting. *There is no Rock* means that for Israel, there is no source of refuge and strength other than God.

Against Idolatry (44:9-20)

This song about the idols and their makers has two parts. Verses 9-12 discuss those who make and worship idols; verses 13-20 discuss the processes by which idols are made.

Verses 14-20 draw an ironic comparison between two different uses of wood. The same tree can be used to fuel a fire and to construct an idol. The idol maker bows down before a piece of wood. Verse 20 quotes a proverb about useless activity to conclude this whole section.

Concluding Words (44:21-23)

Verses 21-23 round off the longer section that began at 42:14. Their theme is the same as that of 44:6-8. God has forgiven the sins of the people. They respond in joy to that proclamation. Verse 23 is a call to praise similar to those in 42:10-13; 45:8; 48:20-21; and 52:9-10.

The message of 44:24-28 will be discussed at the beginning of the next section.

§ § § § § § §

The Message of Isaiah 41—44

§ In the person and work of Cyrus, king of Persia, we can see the hand of Yahweh, the God of Israel.

§ The people were in despair, thinking that their God had forsaken them. Just at the height of their despair, Second Isaiah's message of hope breaks through.

§ God's divinity is shown by the involvement God has had in history. No other gods can make this claim.

§ The people of Israel, summoned by the prophet, respond to God's promise in joy and celebration.

§ At times the people have been blind and deaf to God's message.

§ § § § § § §

Isaiah 45–48

Introduction to These Chapters

This section begins with the so-called Cyrus Oracle (which actually starts at 44:28). Also included in these chapters are two calls to praise, a trial speech, more material concerning idol worship, a lament over Babylon's fate, and various miscellaneous oracles.

Here is an outline of Chapters 45–48.

I. Commission of Cyrus (44:24–45:13)
  A. Introduction (44:24-28)
  B. The Cyrus oracle (45:1-7)
  C. Concluding call to praise (45:8)
  D. The power of God (45:9-13)
II. Miscellaneous Oracles (45:14–46:13)
  A. Oracles concerning the nations (45:14-25)
  B. Address to Israel (46:1-4)
  C. Against idol worship (46:5-8)
  D. Oracle of deliverance (46:9-13)
III. Lament Over Babylon (47:1-15)
IV. God's Actions in History (48:1-22)
  A. Oracle of deliverance (48:1-11)
  B. Oracle of deliverance (48:12-17)
  C. Peace like a river (48:18-19)
  D. Release from Babylon (48:20-22)

Commission of Cyrus (44:24–45:13)

The Cyrus Oracle, found in 45:1-7, is unique among Second Isaiah's prophecies, and also in the Old Testament as a whole. In form it is a royal oracle, similar to those that have been preserved from the annals of some ancient Near Eastern rulers. In content, this oracle is similar to the Cyrus cylinder, an inscription from Cyrus's archives which is still extant. The message of this oracle is that Yahweh, God of Israel, is anointing King Cyrus of Persia to accomplish the task of setting Israel free from captivity. Cyrus will do this by conquering Babylonia and sending its prisoners back to their homeland.

Introduction (44:24-28)

This section, from a grammatical point of view, is nothing more than a series of noun clauses describing the nature and character of God. The descriptions convey the message that God is both creator and lord of history (a common theme in Second Isaiah). The addressees are the people of Israel, all of whom were formed by God while they were still in the womb.

The only real statement made in this section is *I am the Lord;* everything that follows that statement elaborates on what God is like. God created both the world and the people in it, and God decreed the restoration of Jerusalem. God also commissioned Cyrus as an instrument to bring about this restoration.

The Cyrus Oracle (45:1-7)

The oracle proper is contained in verses 1-4. Verses 5-7 begin with the same divine self-predication formula that is found in verse 24 (*I am the Lord*) and elaborate on it by describing what God will accomplish and why.

Whereas the introduction in verses 24-28 addresses Israel, the oracle in verses 1-4 addresses Cyrus, king of Persia. There is no doubt, however, that the message is intended for Israel as well.

Verse 1 reintroduces the oracle to Cyrus with the words *Thus says the Lord to his anointed, to Cyrus.* God's *anointed* is the word for *messiah.* The surprising element of this statement is that God calls a non-Israelite a messiah. This designation indicates the extreme importance of Cyrus's mission. Grasping a king's right hand (verse 1) is part of the coronation ritual for a king. As a result of God's anointing, Cyrus will be able to *subdue nations*.

The last part of verse 3 gives an indication of why God has chosen Cyrus for this mission. The end result will be that Israel will understand that God is working on their behalf.

My servant Jacob and *Israel my chosen* are common designations for God's people throughout Second Isaiah.

Verses 5-7 elaborate on the phrase *I am the Lord*. The purpose is to explain to Cyrus who this God is who has anointed him. According to verse 5, Cyrus does not know who God is. According to verse 7, God is the one who created everything. The statements made here are certainly extravagant. We know from Genesis 1 that the darkness existed before God created the world. The statement that God makes weal and creates woe is disturbing. We must recognize that the prophet is making sweeping statements that are not intended to be taken literally.

Concluding Call to Praise (45:8)

Here the prophet summons the heavens and the earth to sing praise to God. Like the other calls to praise in the book, this call begins with an imperative summons, and then continues by giving the reason for praise. God is worthy of praise because *I the Lord have created it*.

The Power of God (45:9-13)

These verses are a woe oracle. This form is common in Isaiah's prophecies (Chapters 1–39), but is found in only this one instance in the second half of the book. This oracle is addressed to those persons who (apparently) question God's commissioning of Cyrus.

The oracle uses language and imagery that are

characteristic of the wisdom literature. The metaphor of potter and clay conveys the message that human beings (the clay) should not contend with God (the potter).

Verse 11 alludes to the charge these persons have made against God's commissioning of Cyrus. God answers that the accomplishments of the past should speak for themselves and should provide proof that God's intentions are for the good of the chosen people. Verse 13 makes the promise specific—the release of the exiles and the restoration of their homeland.

Oracles Concerning the Nations (45:14-25)

These verses concern the fate of foreign nations such as Egypt and Seba (Arabia). The riches of these nations will be given to Israel, and their people will worship Yahweh, the God of Israel. The prophet even envisions what these people will say when they are converted to worshiping God (see verse 14). Verse 15 makes the point that from now on, God's activity in history will not be understandable to everyone. God's purposes will be hidden.

Verses 16-17 judge those who make idols and describe their fate. It is contrasted with the fate of the people of God, who will be *saved by the Lord*.

Verses 18-19 describe God, the creator of Israel. Contrary to what people say and think, God did not *speak in secret*. Up until now, God's purposes are clear and understandable to everyone.

Verses 20-25 are a trial speech in which God confronts the gods of other nations, especially the gods of Babylonia. Those gods are gods *that cannot save* (verse 20). According to verse 22, it was not just Israel who was involved in future restoration. As a result of God's actions, people from all parts of the earth will be converted to the God of Israel. Verse 23 is quoted in Romans 14:11, where Paul speaks of the final judgment at the end of time.

Address to Israel (46:1-4)

These verses are addressed to the people of Israel, and they concern the Babylonian gods *Bel* and *Nebo*. The images of these gods are apparently being carried away from the temple on the backs of beasts of burden. The prophet sees irony in the fact that these idols cannot support even themselves, much less the people they are supposed to protect. The picture the prophet is painting in these verses is one of the people taking idols out of the temple, loading them onto animals, and taking them away so they will not be stolen or destroyed when the city falls to the Persians.

Verses 3 and 4 contrast the God of Israel with these Babylonian gods. Whereas they are powerless to help their people, and must be carried by them, the God of Israel will carry the people out of exile.

Against Idol Worship (46:5-8)

These verses relate to the other sections of Second Isaiah that discuss idol worship. (See 40:18-20; 44:9-20.) As in the other passages of this type, here the prophet uses irony to make his point. The idols, or images, of other gods can be made by a goldsmith. Who would want to worship something that can be made by common people? Not only that, an idol, once it has been set down, cannot move of its own accord. It must be carried. How can you worship a god who cannot move to help you in times of need?

Oracle of Deliverance (46:9-13)

In these verses, God addresses the people of Israel directly. God reminds them of past accomplishments on their behalf, and then promises to accomplish more in the future. As is characteristic of these prophecies as a whole, the prophet speaks of a future event (the return from exile) as though it had already happened. *The bird of prey from the east* is a reference to Cyrus.

Lament Over Babylon (47:1-15)

This poem is divided into five separate stanzas: (1) verses 1-4, (2) verses 5-7, (3) verses 8-9, (4) verses 10-12, and (5) verses 13-15. In essence, the message of this lament is that Babylon's gods will fail to rescue the people from the Persians. Unlike the people of Israel, the Babylonians do not have a god they can rely on to rescue them.

The first series of imperatives (in verse 1) are addressed to the virgin Babylon, which indicates the height from which the city is about to fall. She has a robe and veil, indicating her (former) exalted status. The prophet allows us to witness the humiliation of the city, which is described in terms of a virgin being defiled. Once humiliated, she will do the work of a slave.

Verses 5-7 continue to address Babylon, commanding her to *sit in silence* and *go into darkness*. *Chaldeans* is another word for *Babylonians*. God was angry with the people of Israel; that is why they were given over to the Babylonians. But the Babylonians treated them harshly, and for that they will be punished, says the Lord. In addition, the Babylonians did not understand that their might came from God rather than from themselves.

Verses 8-9 deliver a message that Babylon is not as secure as the people think it is. For their complacency the people will be punished by childlessness and widowhood, two of the worst possible fates that could befall a woman.

Verses 10-12 indicate that the practices of sorcery, so important to Babylon's culture, will not help the people predict their own fate. Verses 13-15 discuss astrology and how it will not help the Babylonians out of their predicament. Babylon will be burned, and even its allies will not come to help.

Oracle of Deliverance (48:1-11)

For those familiar with the language, style, and tone of Second Isaiah's prophecies, this section will sound harsher than most of the rest of the book. Although the message is consistent with this prophet's theology (God as creator and lord of history), the words that convey the message are unusually judgmental in tone.

The oracle has two parts. The first part (verses 3-5) discusses God's past deeds. The second part of the oracle (verses 6-11) promises future deliverance.

According to verses 1-2, God's people have not been sincere in their response to God. They do not deserve God's protection. The people are stubborn, and attribute God's accomplishments to the power of other gods.

In verses 6-11, the prophet turns his attention to the *new things* God is about to accomplish on Israel's behalf. God will not be angry because of the people's stubbornness. On the contrary, God will not cut them off. The *furnace of afflictions* refers to Israel's period of captivity in Babylon. This same image was used earlier to refer to the time of servitude in Egypt (see Deuteronomy 4:20).

Oracle of Deliverance (48:12-17)

In this oracle addressed directly to the people of Israel, God describes a past accomplishment on their behalf—the creation of the world. Secure in this knowledge, the people should be assured that God will save them from their present circumstances as well. *I have brought him* (verse 15) refers to Cyrus. *Who among them* refers to the Babylonian gods, who are incapable of acts such as the creation of the world. God, on the other hand, intends to lead the people *in the way you should go*, that is, back home to Judah.

Peace Like a River (48:18-19)

These two verses lament the disobedience of the people. If they had obeyed, their sense of contentment and well-being would have been like a gently-flowing river. Their offspring would have been numerous, like the grains of sand on the seashore.

Release From Babylon (48:20-22)

This short section begins with a command to leave Babylon with shouts of joy. Their song of celebration will praise God as the one who has brought it all about. Verse 21 alludes to the first Exodus, when God brought the people out of Egypt.

Verse 22 is an addition, probably placed here because of its mention of peace (corresponding to 48:18-19). This same admonition is repeated in 57:21.

§ § § § § § §

The Message of Isaiah 45–48

These chapters conclude the first half of Second Isaiah's prophecies. What can we learn from the material included in Chapters 45–48 about God and about the chosen people?

§ God has chosen Cyrus, a heathen king, to accomplish great things on behalf of the chosen people.

§ God is seen as protector and supporter of the people of Israel, in contrast to the Babylonian gods who must be carried by their people.

§ Second Isaiah proclaims a message that is positive and hopeful in its entirety.

§ God's goal in releasing the people from their captivity involves not just the people of Israel, but people from all over the earth.

§ § § § § § §

Isaiah 49–52

Introduction to These Chapters

Chapters 49–52 begin the second half of Second Isaiah's prophecies. In this section are two servant songs, several calls to praise, some miscellaneous oracles, and a call to depart from Babylon. Whereas Chapters 40–48 are composed of numerous short oracles and speeches, the second half of the book contains units that are, for the most part, longer and more complex.

Here is an outline of Chapters 49–52.

I. Second Servant Song (49:1-6)
II. Return and Restoration (49:7-26)
  A. Day of salvation (49:7-12)
  B. Call to praise (49:13)
  C. God's love for Israel (49:14-26)
III. Covenant With Israel (50:1-3)
IV. Third Servant Song (50:4-11)
V. Salvation for Abraham's Descendants (51:1-16)
  A. Future deliverance (51:1-8)
  B. Awake! Awake! (51:9-16)
VI. Kingship of God (51:17–52:12)
  A. Restoration of Jerusalem (51:17-23)
  B. Awake! Awake! (52:1-2)
  C. Fate of Israel's enemies (52:3-6)
  D. Future restoration (52:7-12)

Second Servant Song (49:1-6)

This servant song is the second of four; the others are found in 42:1-4; 50:4-9; and 52:13–53:12. In this song, the servant speaks in the first person and addresses the *coastlands* and *peoples from afar*, in other words, the Gentiles. Like the first servant song, this one speaks of God's commissioning of the servant and the servant's mission. (See Jeremiah 1:5.)

Like the prophet Jeremiah, the servant was called by God while he was still inside his mother's womb. Also like the prophets, the servant's call has to do with the words he speaks. His mouth is *like a sharp sword*—the words that come from it will not always be easy to hear, but they will reach their destination. The same thing is said about the words of a prophet in Jeremiah 23:29. The second part of verse 2 indicates that during at least some of his mission the servant worked in secret.

Verse 3 explains the reason for God's commissioning of the servant—so that God might be glorified. In a similar response to that of the prophets when they are called, the servant hesitates, saying that thus far his work has been in vain. He seems to be reassuring himself in the second half of verse 4. God is still with him, protecting him and guiding him as he works.

Verses 5 and 6 contrast Israel in the past with the restored land. Verse 5 introduces the saying with a series of phrases describing God's calling of the servant. Verse 6 expands the servant's mission from Israel to the nations, *to the ends of the earth.*

Day of Salvation (49:7-12)

This section relates to the servant song that immediately precedes it. This construction is similar to 42:1-9 (servant song in 42:1-4 followed by a related speech in verses 5-9). God is here speaking in the first person, addressing Israel concerning the coming day of salvation. The word *servant* is repeated in verse 7, making the connection with verses 1-6.

Verses 8-12 describe the release of the captives and the victorious journey home. Their present situation is described as being in darkness, but that situation is about to change for the better. God will guide the people on their way, just as in the Exodus out of Egypt. The land of Syene is south of Egypt.

Call to Praise (49:13)

This whole section is concluded by a call to praise in 49:13. It is similar in structure and content to the other calls to praise in Second Isaiah. (See 42:10-13; 44:23; 45:8; 52:9-10.) *The Lord has comforted his people* echoes the opening words of the book in 40:1.

God's Love for Israel (49:14-26)

This section begins with a quote that probably comes directly from a community lament. The people have complained that God has forsaken them. In the verses that follow, God maintains that this is not the case at all. Just as a mother loves her newborn baby, God loves the people of Israel. In fact, there is a greater chance that the mother will forget her child than that God will forget the people.

God has *graven* (engraved) *you on the palm of my hands*, like a tattoo. Verse 18 portrays the restored Jerusalem as magnificent and adorned. The returned exiles will be like jewels that adorn the city.

Verses 20-22 continue the description of the restored city. The people will become so numerous that the city will not be large enough to hold them all. *Children born in the time of your bereavement* are those born during the Babylonian Exile. Although the people thought (while they were exiled) that they were barren, they were wrong.

Verse 23 uses the image of God raising a signal. Usually such signals indicate that it is time to launch an attack. Here, however, God's raising of a hand signals that it is time to depart from Babylon and return home to Judah. Along the way home, former enemies will bow down and lick the dust off the feet of the people of Israel. The ultimate goal is the glorification of Israel's God (verse 23). And in verse 26 the goal is extended to *all flesh*.

Covenant With Israel (50:1-3)

According to the message of these verses, Israel is not divorced from God, nor is Israel sold into slavery. God's protection is constant. Verse 2 asks a series of rhetorical questions to which the implied answer is *no*.

Third Servant Song (50:4-11)

As is the case with the servant song in 49:1-6, this song points out the similarities between the mission of the servant and the ministry of Israel's prophets. The servant speaks in the first person, addressing the people of Israel.

In verse 4, the servant says that God *has given me the tongue of those who are taught*—in other words, the servant knows how to communicate the message he is given to proclaim. He proclaims this message to the weary exiles who are in need of words of comfort. *Morning by morning* means that God tells the servant not only what to say, but also when to say it.

The servant was obedient, and did what God told him to do (verse 5). However, the people did not respond positively to the message. The fact that the servant had to suffer physical abuse at the hands of his audience did not deter him from accomplishing his mission. Why? Because God is on the side of the servant (verse 7). His sincere conviction is symbolized by his setting his face like stone.

In verses 8-9, the servant uses legal process to convince his audience that God is on his side. Those who oppose the servant are summoned to state their case. The fact that they are silent proves the truth of the servant's conviction.

Verses 10-11 are an addition to the servant song. They pick up its message, stating that the servant will walk in darkness but will remain steadfast in his trust of God. True light comes only from God. Those who light their own fires will be punished for their faithlessness.

Future Deliverance (51:1-8)

This addition to the servant song in 50:4-11 (although separated from it by verses 7-9) is similar to the additions to the two previous servant songs (see 42:5-9 and 49:7-12).

These verses are a first-person address by God to the people of Israel, who *seek the Lord* and want to be delivered from their present circumstances. Just as God once called Abraham and Sarah and promised them many descendants (see Genesis 12:1-3), God will act now on behalf of the chosen people. Verse 3 elaborates on what God will do, using the Garden of Eden as a symbol of God's creation. Just as Eden was the perfect situation at the beginning of time, restored Judah will be a place of comfort for the returning exiles.

Verses 4-6 are introduced by an imperative commanding the people to listen; this verb corresponds to *hearken* in verse 1. Law and justice will proceed from God, as well as salvation and deliverance. Although earthly things are transitory, God's protection will endure forever. This idea is expressed also in Isaiah 40:31.

Verses 7-9 form the third part of this section, and they begin with the same imperative that began verse 1. The message of this section is a restatement of the content of verses 4-6.

Awake! Awake! (51:9-16)

This section is a lament raised by the people and spoken to God. Like other portions of Second Isaiah's prophecies, these words may be a direct quote from a community lament used during services of worship.

The people ask God to come to their aid just as in the past acts of creation. Verses 9 and 10 use imagery from ancient Babylonian creation myths to describe God's creation of the earth, protraying the creation a little differently than it is described in Genesis 1.

Verse 11 is quoted almost word for word in Isaiah 35:10. The *ransomed of the Lord* are those exiles who are destined to return to their homeland.

Verses 12-16 give God's answer to the community lament found in verses 9-11. Yes, God will again intervene in Israel's history. Do not be afraid that God will forsake you. God, the same God who created the heavens and earth, will rescue the people from their distress.

Restoration of Jerusalem (51:17-23)

This section begins with a double imperative, *Rouse yourself, rouse yourself,* spoken by God and directed to the city of Jerusalem. This technique is quite common in Second Isaiah's writings, and it indicates the urgency he felt in delivering his message to the exiles.

The inhabitants of Jerusalem *have drunk to the dregs the bowl of staggering;* in other words, they have experienced the wrath of God to the extent that they are hopelessly downtrodden and despondent. However, verses 21-23 turn the tables. Now the enemies of Israel will be humiliated, and Israel will be exalted. The reason for this reversal is given in verse 23: Israel's enemies have treated the people shamefully.

Awake! Awake! (52:1-2)

Again we see the double imperative, directed to Jerusalem from the mouth of God. Jerusalem is commanded to adorn herself with garments and with strength. The uncircumcised (non-Jews) and the (ritually) unclean will no longer pass through Jerusalem's gates. These undesirables symbolize Israel's enemies, who will pay for the injustices they have committed against Israel.

Shake yourself from the dust means to start a new

existence in totally different circumstances. We often say *shake the dust off your feet* when advising someone to start living life differently.

Fate of Israel's Enemies (52:3-6)

This section is prose rather than poetry. It discusses Israel's enemies in some detail, and so is related in content to the preceding verses. The passage begins by describing Israel's bondage in Egypt, and then moves to the period of Assyrian domination. Finally the prophet mentions the Babylonian captivity (*my people are taken away*). *Their rulers wail* does not have an obvious meaning in this context. Perhaps they are already bemoaning their future fate.

The last verse gives the message of the section: God wants everyone to *know my name,* in other words, to know the Lord intimately.

Future Restoration (52:7-12)

This is a very famous passage depicting the imminent release of the captives, proclaimed by a messenger. *Beautiful* refers not so much to the messenger's feet but to the message he proclaims. That this messenger's feet land on the mountains (surrounding Jerusalem) indicates that the prophet is speaking of the return as though it had already taken place.

Verse 8 portrays the anticipation the people felt; they are watching and waiting for the sign to depart. They are so certain of their imminent departure that they sing for joy together.

Verses 9-10 are a call to praise. Their structure is similar to that of 42:10-13; 44:23; 45:8; 49:13. Whereas in the previous verse the watchmen were singing together, here all the waste places of Jerusalem join in as well. The second half of verse 9 gives the reason for the call to praise. God has comforted the people. This statement is elaborated on in verse 10.

Verses 11-12 are the culmination of all the prophet's words thus far. It is now time for the people to depart. They are to purify themselves as they would to prepare for a service of worship. They are to *bear the vessels of the Lord* back to Jerusalem. God as protector of the people and bringer of salvation will be revealed to everyone as a result of this new exodus from Babylon.

Note: 52:13-15 will be discussed at the beginning of Part Eighteen.

§ § § § § § §

The Message of Isaiah 49–52

What do these chapters tell us about God and about God's relationship to the people in exile?

§ God is in control of history and everything that happens in history.

§ God maintained (and will continue to maintain) a close relationship with the people, even though they do not deserve God's continued protection.

§ God remains faithful to the covenant formerly established with the people of Israel.

§ The servant is able to continue his mission, even though it seems to be unprofitable, because he is assured of the continuing presence of God.

§ Persons who do not treat the people of God with justice and righteousness will be punished for their attitude.

§ That God intends to uphold the covenant obligations with the people is evidenced by the fact that God has kept the promises made earlier to Abraham.

§ § § § § § §

Isaiah 53–55

Introduction to These Chapters

Chapters 53–55 are the final three chapters in the book of Second Isaiah, the prophet of the Babylonian Exile. They are followed by a collection of prophecies from the post-exilic period, from the hand of an anonymous prophet called Third Isaiah (Chapters 56–66). Isaiah 53–55 includes the fourth servant song, a call to praise, a proclamation of salvation, a conclusion to the book, and other miscellaneous oracles.

Here is an outline of these chapters.

I. Fourth Servant Song (52:13–53:12)
   A. God speaks (52:13-15)
   B. Others speak (53:1-10)
   C. God speaks (53:11-12)
II. Assurance of Israel's Restoration (54:1-17)
   A. Summons to sing (54:1-10)
   B. Future salvation (54:11-17)
III. Song of Triumph (55:1-13)
   A. Restoration of Judah (55:1-5)
   B. Epilogue (55:6-13)

Fourth Servant Song (52:13–53:12)

The fourth servant song is one of the most well-known passages in Scripture. The fourth song should be read in the context of the first three songs (see 42:1-4; 49:1-6; and 50:4-11), and should be seen as the climax of the message proclaimed in these earlier songs. This fourth song is divided into three parts, according to who is speaking.

The song includes three verses from Chapter 52, and all of Chapter 53.

God Speaks (52:13-15)

The fourth servant song begins with a speech by God. The concluding words (verses 11b-12 of Chapter 53) are also spoken by God. These introductory and concluding words form the frame for the speech by an unidentified group of people (53:1-11a).

God opens the speech in verses 13-15 with a description of the servant as *exalted and lifted up.* The description is introduced by the words *Behold, my servant.* These same words, uttered by God, are used to introduce the first servant song in Isaiah 42:1-4. The description of the servant's high status stands in direct contrast to his physical appearance, which God describes in verse 14. *His appearance was so marred* that he looked almost inhuman. As a result of his horrifying appearance, he will *startle many nations.*

As the RSV indicates, the meaning of the Hebrew verb translated *startle* is uncertain. When it is used elsewhere in the Old Testament it means to leap; perhaps here nations will leap, figuratively, as a result of being startled. The reaction of kings and nations to the servant's accomplishments and his physical appearance is reminiscent again of the first servant song in 42:1-4.

The last two lines of verse 15 make clear that the mission of the servant is unique. Nothing like this has ever happened before. These words are quoted directly in Romans 15:21, where Paul is discussing the newness of the gospel message.

Others Speak (53:1-11)

In this section of the song, a group of people begin describing the servant's life history, and lamenting his current situation. They begin by stating that he grew up in relatively normal circumstances. He did not stand out so that he would be noticed by others. *Like a young plant* is language similar to that used in many messianic prophecies. For example, Isaiah 11:1 speaks of a shoot from the stump of Jesse. (See also Jeremiah 23:5.)

In verse 3 the description of the servant moves from his appearance to his humiliation. Using language that reminds us of the lament psalms, this unidentified group of people portray the servant's whole life as dominated by suffering. Many of the words used in verse 3 have uncertain meanings, but the general tone and message are clear. The servant has been humiliated and rejected by his community.

Verses 4-6 turn our attention to the attitude that persons had about this servant. Whereas in verse 3 the servant was rejected, in verse 4 the speakers seem to come to the realization that his humiliation was actually on their behalf. *Borne our griefs* might also be translated *borne our sickness; carried our sorrows* might be translated *carried our pains.*

After coming to the realization that the servant's humiliation and rejection were for their sake, these persons respond by a kind of confession that they have turned away from God (verse 6). The servant, in his own quiet way, has atoned for these sins.

The idea of suffering in silence is continued in verses 7-9. Even though the servant was *oppressed* and *afflicted,* he did not open his mouth to complain. He is likened to a lamb who is being taken to be slaughtered. Verses 7 and 8 make the point that even in the face of violence perpetrated by others (*stricken; cut off*) the servant did not waver.

The second half of verse 8 and all of verse 9 describe the death and burial of the servant. He was buried with evildoers, thus continuing the atmosphere of suffering and shame that surrounded him. *And with a rich man in his death* (verse 9) might also be translated *and his tomb with evildoers.* This latter translation makes better sense since it parallels the first phrase in the verse.

Verses 10-12 describe the servant's deliverance from his former state. God, who was involved in the servant's situation from the beginning (verse 10), has intervened and turned his circumstances around. But what does God's intervention really mean? Was the servant resurrected from the dead? The text is vague at this point. It is clear, however, that as a result of the change in his circumstances the servant will prosper in the future. *He shall see his offspring* is a Hebrew way of saying that he will live a full life. A large family was a sign of prosperity and God's blessings.

God Speaks (53:11-12)

God is speaking in the first person, as in the introductory words in verses 13-15 of Chapter 52. Thus the fourth servant song begins and ends with what God has to proclaim. The last part of verse 12 summarizes the servant's mission. *He bore the sin of many, and made intercession for the transgressors.*

Assurance of Israel's Restoration (54:1-17)

All of Chapter 54 has but one theme: the future restoration of Israel. A note of triumph prevails throughout the whole chapter. Verses 1-10 are a summons to sing a restoration song, and verses 11-17 are a description of future salvation, centering on the city of Jerusalem.

Summons to Sing (54:1-10)

This song is addressed to *the barren one, who did not bear*—a metaphor for the people of Israel in exile. The introductory summons to sing in verses 1-3 sounds similar to the calls to praise found elsewhere in Second Isaiah (see 42:10; 44:23).

In ancient Israel, being barren was one of the worst possible fates for a woman. Dread of barrenness was caused largely by the fact that many children were considered to indicate God's blessing upon a married couple. Lack of children could therefore cause misery and even shame, especially on the part of the woman. In this passage, the prophet uses the image of the barren woman to refer to the people as a whole. They were miserable, and felt defeated and ashamed.

There is an ironic twist to the prophet's words. Why would a barren woman (or exiled Israel) want to break forth into singing? What possible reason would she have to rejoice? Why would she want to enlarge her house (verse 2) since she had no children to inhabit it? The answer is given in verse 3. *Your descendants will possess the nations.* You will return to inhabit the *desolate cities* of Judah.

Verses 4-6 continue the references to Israel's shame, but they promise that the shame will not continue. The *shame of your youth* (their disobedience) will give way to a bright future in restored Jerusalem. Verses 5-6 use the image of God as husband and Israel as wife. The prophet Hosea uses similar imagery to proclaim his message (see Hosea 2; 11). God, the husband, promises not to reject his wife.

In verses 7-10 the prophet compares the experience of the Exile with Noah's experience when the earth was destroyed. He also compares the promise of return from the Exile to the covenant God made with Noah never to destroy the earth again. The words of verse 10 must have sounded restorative and comforting to the people in exile.

Future Salvation (54:11-17)

These verses open with an address to the *afflicted one*. A similar address is found in Isaiah 51:21. Here again, an individual is used to represent the entire community. What follows the introduction is a description of what will happen to Jerusalem (the afflicted one) when she is being restored. The city will be rebuilt with precious stones forming its foundation.

According to verses 13-15, the city's people, as well as its foundations, will be restored. They will be well educated, many in number, obedient to God, and free from fear and oppression. God promises to protect the inhabitants of Jerusalem from all outside enemies.

Song of Triumph (55:1-13)

The song of triumph is a fitting way to conclude this major section in the Book of Isaiah, which began at 40:1. The song is in two parts. Verses 1-5 describe the restoration of Judah, and verses 6-13 are a kind of epilogue that summarizes the message of this prophet of the Exile.

Restoration of Judah (55:1-5)

This song is introduced by the word *Ho*, which is used to get the attention of the hearers. What follows is a series of imperatives, a technique often used throughout Chapters 40–55. (See 51:17; 52:1, 11; 54:1.) These imperatives are different from others in these prophecies because they summon the audience to eat and drink. This kind of summons is similar to those found in the wisdom literature, that call persons to a banquet. (For example, see Proverbs 9:3-6.) Here the summons is not to an actual banquet, but to a restored community. The people are summoned so that their souls might live (verse 3).

Verses 3-5 remind the readers of God's earlier covenant with David, in which God promised David, and Israel, steadfast love forever. Psalm 89 discusses a similar theme. When Judah is restored and the people return to dwell there, life will be so abundant that others from distant lands will come to live there, too.

Epilogue (55:6-13)

This section has many similarities to Chapter 40, which introduces this section of Isaiah. Together, Chapter 40 and Chapter 55 form a frame for these prophecies.

(Compare the message of 55:11 to that of 40:8.)

This epilogue begins with an admonition to seek God, to return to God in humility and ask forgiveness. Verses 9-10 praise God as creator, whose word brings new life to persons just as rain brings fertility to the ground.

Verses 11-12 are a fitting conclusion to this section of the book, since they sum up all parts of the prophet's message. The people will return to their homeland. There will be great rejoicing on the journey home. God will be praised as the one who has brought it all about.

§ § § § § § §

The Message of Isaiah 53–55

These are important chapters in Isaiah, since they contain the fourth servant song and they also conclude a major section of the book. They provide insight into the message of Chapters 40–55.

§ God can work wonders through unlikely persons.

§ Proclaiming God's word is not always an easy task. Sometimes suffering is the result.

§ God's will is not always clear to us, but God can accomplish whatever is intended.

§ Trust in God will bring its own rewards, even though it is difficult to recognize what those rewards will be.

§ God will love us steadfastly, and will not forsake us. The covenant assures us of God's continued presence.

§ God's thoughts and ways are not our thoughts and ways.

§ A return to restored Jerusalem is a return to a right relationship with God.

§ § § § § § §

Introduction to Isaiah 56–66

Chapters 56–66 form the third major portion of Isaiah. Many commentators maintain that this final section was written by yet a third prophet, a disciple of Second Isaiah in Jerusalem during the early years of the restoration. This unknown prophet is often called *Third Isaiah*.

Chapters 56–66 can be dated most probably sometime during the fourth century B.C. Five main characteristics suggest a late date for these prophecies. First, these chapters share many words and themes with the words of the prophets Haggai and Zechariah, who also lived and worked during the fourth century B.C. Second, spread throughout these chapters is an interest in eschatology, or the events surrounding the last days. In general, eschatology is an interest of later biblical writers.

Third, this prophet seems to take the content and themes of Second Isaiah and expand on them, adding his own interpretations. For example, the idea of making preparations to return to the homeland, central to the message of Second Isaiah, is taken up and altered slightly in Chapters 56–66. There it is the persons inside the gates of Jerusalem who are to make preparations for those who are yet to return (not the exiles in Babylon, who are addressed in Chapters 40–55).

Fourth, the themes of cultic worship and ritual, virtually absent in the prophecies of Second Isaiah, play a major role in the theology of Chapters 56–66. And fifth, these final chapters emphasize the universality of the message of salvation, which is largely a later phenomenon in the Scripture.

Chapters 60–62 form the heart of this prophet's message. The rest of the oracles in this third portion of Isaiah are a mixture of the prophet's own words and prophecies adapted from other places in the Scripture.

PART NINETEEN Isaiah 56–59

Introduction to These Chapters

Isaiah 56–59 begins the third major portion of the Book of Isaiah. This third section is a collection of prophecies from the post-exilic period (after the return from exile in 538 B.C.). In these first four chapters the prophet speaks against the nation's political leaders and against the practices of idolatry, and he offers a poem of consolation and a summons to repent.

Here is an outline of these chapters.

I. Keeping the Sabbath (56:1-8)
II. Oracle Against Leaders (56:9-12)
III. Oracle Against Idolatry (57:1-13)
IV. Consolation for Israel (57:14-21)
V. What the Lord Desires (58:1-14)
VI. Call to Repentance (59:1-21)

Keeping the Sabbath (56:1-8)

This oracle is introduced by a formula commonly used to introduce prophetic oracles: *Thus says the LORD*. As a whole, this section blesses those who keep the sabbath, that is, who obey the sabbath laws. A similar theme is discussed in 58:13-14. (See also Jeremiah 17:19-27.)

The words *blessed is the man* (verse 2) remind us of Psalm 1:1, a wisdom psalm.

Verse 2 mentions two kinds of behavior that are to be blessed: the keeping of the sabbath and keeping one's *hand from doing any evil*. The first admonition is specific and the second is more general.

Verses 3-8 focus on two elements in Israelite society: the foreigner and the eunuch. The foreigner (see verses 3 and 6) was an alien, a non-Israelite, but who has now joined the worshiping community (see 60:10; 61:5; 62:8). Another word for this kind of person is *proselyte*. The eunuch was formerly an outcast. He was not allowed to participate in Israelite worship. (See Deuteronomy 23:1.) Here the prophet indicates a change in Israel's thinking. Formerly excluded from the worshiping community, these two groups may now participate freely. The only conditions for participation are that they keep the sabbath and obey the covenant.

The promise made to foreigners and eunuchs as they join the community is found in verses 5 and 7-8. Their posterity does not depend on physical offspring. God will make them a memorial—*an everlasting name which shall not be cut off.* The Temple in Jerusalem will become *a house of prayer for all peoples.* This same promise is made in 60:4-7.

Oracle Against Leaders (56:9-12)

In graphic detail, the prophet speaks against the corrupt leaders in Jerusalem. They will be devoured by wild beasts. As in Ezekiel (see 3:17 and 34:10), the terms *watchmen* and *shepherds also designate leaders. These leaders are guilty on two counts. First, they are all dumb dogs,* that is, they cannot act effectively as spokesmen for the community. They would rather sleep. Second, these leaders have acted in their own interests rather than the interests of the people. For these sins they will be punished.

Oracle Against Idolatry (57:1-13)

This oracle begins with a description of what happens to a righteous man when he dies. No one notices that he is gone. *They rest in their beds* (verse 2) means they have died and are now in their graves.

Verse 3 begins a direct address to the *sons of the sorceress,* the ones who do not notice the righteous.

According to the prophet, these corrupt leaders are the ones who should die unnoticed. They are summoned to *draw near* and hear the accusation against them.

In form this section is similar to the trial speeches in Isaiah 41:1-5, 21-29; 43:8-15; 45:20-25. Following the summons (in verse 3) comes the accusation (verses 4-5) and the judgment (verse 6). Verses 7-13 elaborate on the accusation made in verses 4-5.

Verses 7 and 8 describe the immorality that was prevalent in the worship practices of those being accused. On a *high and lofty mountain* refers to the high places where much of the cultic worship took place. *Molech* (verse 9), which could also be translated as *Melek*, or *King*, is probably the name of a Canaanite fertility god. Use of this ancient name and allusions to Canaanite worship practices indicate an early date for this material.

Sheol (verse 9) is the name for the underworld, the habitation of the dead.

Verses 11-12 give the judgment for these idolatrous practices. Because other gods were worshiped, God will not come to their rescue. God is saying that these other gods will be powerless to help them and that God, the only one who can really help them, will not help. With irony, God says: *Let your collection of idols deliver you!*

The second half of verse 13 contrasts the fate of the righteous to the judgment on idolaters. Those who put their trust in God will be rewarded.

Consolation for Israel (57:14-21)

This oracle sounds similar to those in Chapters 40–55. Its message is one of comfort. The oracle is introduced using language reminiscent of Second Isaiah: *Prepare the way*. Repetition of the imperatives in verse 14 is a device used often in Chapters 40–55. (See 40:1; 52:1 11.) Also, the message of comfort, of God's anger being only temporary, sounds like the words of Second Isaiah.

In verse 15, the prophet makes the point that God is at the same time far away (*inhabits eternity*) and close at hand (*with him who is of a contrite and humble spirit*).

Verses 16-21 make the point that God's anger is only temporary. After all, God created life itself, and so cannot continue to be angry with the chosen people. The sentiment expressed here is similar to Second Isaiah's words in 54:7-8.

Verse 17 explains why God is angry. *Because of the iniquity of his (Israel's) covetousness* God became angry and punished the people. But still Israel did not listen. Verse 18 brings a message of comfort. Even though Israel did not respond in faith, God will not continue the punishment. God will comfort *the mourners* (those who repent of their sins). *The fruit of the lips* of these mourners refers to their prayers to God asking forgiveness.

Verses 20-21 contrast the fate of the wicked to those who will receive God's comfort (the mourners). The wicked will have no peace and no rest. Verse 21 is repeated in Isaiah 48:18; in both places it is probably a gloss—a comment by a later reader.

What the Lord Desires (58:1-14)

This message is similar to that of Micah 6:6-8. God requires of the people not fasting or other rituals, but right relationships with each other and with God.

The introductory words in verse 1 give the impression that the speaker is standing before a group of people. Trumpets were usually used to announce the beginning of special days, such as days of fasting. Verse 3 makes specific the intention of the assembly—the people are preparing for a fast. However, according to the prophet, the people are fasting in the wrong spirit and for the wrong reasons (verses 6-9). Fasting should have to do with justice in relationships with others, not with empty ritual.

Verses 9b-12 promise God's presence and guidance if the people remove wickedness from their midst. Gloom will be taken away (verse 10), the people will be happy and healthy (verse 11), and their city will be rebuilt (verse 12).

Verses 13-14 advise the people to observe the rules and regulations related to the sabbath, according to the fourth commandment (see Exodus 20:8-11). *Doing your pleasure* may also be translated *doing your business*. After the people returned from the Exile, observing the sabbath became more and more important in the life of the community. Apparently, the people were becoming lax and the prophet believed they needed a warning. The warning, however, is couched in words of promise. If they will obey the sabbath laws, the people will be rewarded.

To be fed *with the heritage of Jacob* means to enjoy the fruits of the land that was given to their ancestors.

Call to Repentance (59:1-21)

This chapter speaks of Israel's sin and need for repentance. At times the prophet is speaking (verses 1-8, 15*b*-19), sometimes the people speak (verses 9-15*a*), and at the conclusion God speaks (verses 20-21). The themes of a community lament seem to dominate the chapter.

In verses 1-8, the prophet speaks of the charges against the nation of Israel. *Your iniquities have made a separation* refers to the fact that the people have broken their covenant with God because of their sins. *Your hands are defiled with blood* (verse 3) is reminiscent of Isaiah 1:15, where the same charge is made.

Verses 3-8 are a catalogue of Israel's sins: The people have lied, cheated, been deceitful, shed innocent blood, and done other acts of violence.

According to verses 9-15, the people realize that their present circumstances are due to their own evil ways. They speak in the first-person plural, likening themselves to blind persons who cannot find their way. Verse 12 makes use of words used in services of worship at the time this prophecy was written (fifth century B.C.). The statements made by the people are sweeping ones. Society is totally corrupt.

In verses 15b-19, the prophet speaks again. The message is that God, seeing the people's wickedness, decided to intervene when no one else would. God is portrayed as a warrior (see also Isaiah 42:13). Verses 18-19 are similar in content and tone to the message of Second Isaiah (see 41:5; 45:6, for example).

Verse 21 is an oracle from God which promises God's continuing presence and guidance. It is similar to the words in 66:22-23.

§ § § § § § §

The Message of Isaiah 56–59

These chapters are more difficult to read and interpret than some others in the Book of Isaiah. What can we learn from them about God and God's people?

§ Some rituals and regulations are useful and pleasing to God if they are performed in the right spirit.

§ Worship of God is available to everyone.

§ Community leaders have an obligation to guide the people with integrity. Punishment results if that obligation is not taken seriously.

§ Sometimes the deeds and virtues of the righteous go unnoticed.

§ God's anger is not endless; forgiveness is possible.

§ Justice and righteousness are more pleasing to God than fasting or other rituals, especially if the right attitude does not accompany the performance of ritual.

§ There are times when the nation as a whole needs to repent and ask God's forgiveness.

§ § § § § § §

PART
TWENTY **Isaiah 60–62**

Introduction to These Chapters

Chapters 60–62 are similar in content and themes to
Chapters 40–55. These chapters are inspiring and
uplifting. They speak of a glorious future for God's
people as they inhabit a restored Jerusalem.

Here is an outline of Chapters 60–62.

I. Jerusalem's Restoration (60:10-22)
   A. Zion will arise (60:1-3)
   B. The people will return (60:4-9)
   C. Jerusalem will be restored (60:10-16)
   D. Future salvation (60:17-22)
II. The Prophet's Mission to Zion (61:1-11)
   A. The Spirit of the Lord (61:1-3)
   B. God will bring salvation (61:4-11)
III. Zion Is Vindicated (62:1-12)
   A. A new name for Zion (62:1-5)
   B. The watchmen prepare (62:6-12)

Zion Will Arise (60:1-3)

This section opens with a set of imperative verbs
summoning the people to *arise and shine*. Double
imperatives are characteristic of Second Isaiah's style (see
51:17, for example). The only difference is that when this
device is used in Chapters 56–66, two different verbs are
placed one after the other. In Chapters 40–55, the same
verb is usually used twice in a row.

The glory of the Lord (verse 1) alludes to God's majesty;
the phrase is common in Ezekiel (see 10:4). The light that

142   ISAIAH

has come to the people is contrasted to the darkness which formerly surrounded them. This contrast is reminiscent of Isaiah 9, where the messianic king is described in terms of a light shining in the darkness.

The People Will Return (60:4-9)

In verse 4, the people are summoned to look around them and see the people returning to Jerusalem. Those summoned are the people who have already returned to the city. Clearly, many persons had not yet returned from Babylon; they are the objects of the prophet's words in these verses. The sight of a vast throng of people returning home will thrill the people who have already arrived. Not only will the rest of the people return, they will bring their wealth with them.

Six nations are mentioned in verses 6-9. Midian is a territory directly east of the Gulf of Aqabah; Ephah is a portion of Midian. Sheba is south of Midian; its queen came to visit King Solomon (see 1 Kings 10). Kedar is mentioned in Isaiah 21:16; it is a territory in northern Arabia. Nebaioth is in Arabia as well; both Kedar and Nebaioth are listed in Genesis 25:13 as sons of Ishmael. Tarshish is a colony in southern Spain.

The last part of verse 9 says that through this glorious return of the people, God will be glorified.

Jerusalem Will Be Restored (60:10-16)

Verse 10 begins a new section that describes what this new era of salvation will be like. Jerusalem will be rebuilt by *foreigners*, who, ironically, destroyed the city some 100 years earlier. The second half of verse 10 quotes Isaiah 54:8.

Verse 12 proclaims that those nations who do not serve the restored Israel will be destroyed. Verses 13-14 describe the rebuilding of the Temple in Jerusalem (*my sanctuary*). It will be rebuilt using wood from Lebanon, which was also used to build the first Temple (see 1 Kings 5). According to verses 15-16, Jerusalem will no longer be forsaken, but will be *majestic forever*. All this will take place in order that God may be known as the Lord among all nations. This language is reminiscent of Isaiah 45:6.

Future Salvation (60:17-22)

These verses describe a momentous change that will soon take place in restored Jerusalem. Outwardly the city will look better than it did before. Bronze and iron will be replaced with silver and gold. Wood and stones will be replaced with bronze and iron. Inwardly, even more important changes will occur. The people will turn to God.

Verses 19-21 focus on the glory of God. *Your God will be your glory* (verse 19) means that even the light in the restored city will come from God. The people will not need the sun and moon to provide light.

Your days of mourning shall be ended (verse 20) is this prophet's way of stating what Second Isaiah said in Chapter 40: *her warfare is ended* (40:2).

The proclamation that concludes this chapter (*I am the* LORD) assures the prophet's audience that what is proclaimed will actually come to pass.

The Spirit of the Lord (61:1-3)

These three verses reveal more about the prophet responsible for Chapters 56–66 than any other portion of the book. Parts of these verses are quoted by Jesus in Luke 4:18-19, as he describes his calling by God. This passage is similar in tone to Second Isaiah's servant songs (see 42:1-4, for example).

According to verse 1, God has *anointed* the prophet to bring *good news to the afflicted* (this last word could also be translated *poor*). Elsewhere in the Old Testament, anointing is usually reserved for kings. Here, however, the prophet is anointed. He is given full authority to speak for God.

The concept of a *day of vengeance* is found in Isaiah 34:8 and 63:4, and in Jeremiah 46:10. In each case the general meaning is not revenge, but rather a change of circumstance.

The word *comfort* appears at the end of verse 2. Whereas in Chapters 40–55 it is the people who are to be comforted, here in 61:2 it is the *mourners*.

God Will Bring Salvation (61:4-11)

Verses 4-11 elaborate on how the people's situation will be changed when they reside in restored Jerusalem. The city will be rebuilt both physically (verse 4) and in the hearts and minds of its inhabitants (verse 7).

The word *build* is common in Chapters 56–66 (see 58:12; 65:21, 22), since the rebuilding of Jerusalem is the main theme of these final chapters in Isaiah.

You shall be called the priests of the LORD (verse 6) is reminiscent of the promise made to the Israelites in Exodus 19:5-6. Those who will inhabit the restored city will be *priests*, in contrast to aliens and foreigners who will be their servants. These priests will receive double their portion, echoing the earlier words of Second Isaiah (see 40:2).

I hate robbery and wrong (verse 8) could also be translated *robbery with a burnt offering*, according to the note in the Revised Standard Version. Verse 9 gives the reason behind the restoration of the city: so that all nations will acknowledge that God has blessed Jerusalem.

Verses 10-11 make the point that God's care for the people and their city is as sure as *the earth brings forth its shoots*. Verse 10 sounds like the calls to praise common in Isaiah 40–55 (see 42:10-13). Verse 11 elaborates on the theme of verse 9, that God will bless the restored city and those who dwell in it.

A New Name for Zion (62:1-5)

The prophet continues to speak in the first person. *Zion* and *Jerusalem* are in parallel clauses; both names designate the city of Jerusalem. The prophet makes it clear that he was not sent to keep silent; he must speak.

Verse 2 promises that Zion/Jerusalem will be *called by a new name* provided by God. A new name is more than a superficial change—it is a new situation. A similar promise is made to Jerusalem in Isaiah 1:26. Verses 4 and 5 specify what the new names will be, and what these names mean.

The Watchmen Prepare (62:6-12)

Verse 6 mentions *watchmen* that will be placed on Jerusalem's walls *all the day and all the night*. *Watchmen* are also mentioned in Isaiah 52:8 and Ezekiel 33; they probably refer to prophets. These watchmen/prophets will remind the people that the city is about to be restored.

Verses 8-9 state that the people will begin to enjoy the fruits of their labors after they return to the restored city. This is in contrast to what has happened during the Exile.

Verses 10-12 summarize the message of this prophet, using language similar to Chapters 40–55. What is different here, however, is that those being summoned are not the exiles in Babylon, but rather those who have already returned to Jerusalem and are living inside the city walls. They are summoned to open the gates so that those who have yet to return will be able to enter the city.

§ § § § § § §

The Message of Isaiah 60–62

§ God's people can shed light on the rest of the world.

§ God will be glorified by the return of the people.

§ With the blessing of God, the chosen people will stand out among all other people.

§ God's blessing can change circumstances dramatically.

§ God can bring about radical changes by a mere utterance.

§ § § § § § §

Isaiah 63–66

Introduction to These Chapters

These chapters form the conclusion to the prophecies in the third portion of the Book of Isaiah, and to the Book of Isaiah as a whole. They contain an oracle proclaiming God's vengeance, an intercessory psalm, an oracle giving God's answer to the request, and several unrelated concluding oracles.

Here is an outline of Isaiah 63–66.

I. God's Vengeance (63:1-6)
II. The Prophet Petitions God (63:7–64:12)
   A. The Exodus from Egypt (63:7-14)
   B. The prophet's request (63:15–64:12)
III. God Answers (65:1-25)
   A. The people rebelled (65:1-7)
   B. God's servants (65:8-16)
   C. New heavens and a new earth (65:17-25)
IV. Final Oracles (66:1-24)
   A. Worship in the Temple (66:1-6)
   B. Jerusalem will rejoice (66:7-16)
   C. The glory of God (66:17-24)

God's Vengeance (63:1-6)

In verse 1, the prophet speaks as one who is watching from the city wall to see who comes and goes through the gates of the city. (He had been given this duty in 62:6.) The one who *comes from Edom*, in splendor and strength, is none other than God, according to the end of verse 1. The image of God trampling grapes (the people) is found also in Joel 3:13.

Verse 2 raises the question of why God's garments are crimson; that question is answered in verse 3. God was angry at the disobedience of the people, and trampled them as punishment. Verses 1-6 explain God's attitude further.

The Exodus From Egypt (63:7-14)

These verses form the first part of a longer section in which the prophet pleads with God to intercede on behalf of the people. As a whole, 63:7–64:11 is a community lament, similar to those in the Psalter, that was probably used by the community in services of worship.

The lament is introduced in verse 7 by a summons to remember God's accomplishments in history. In verse 8, Israel's calling as a covenant people is described. The people's response was to have been faithfulness and obedience. According to verse 9, God protected the people from their enemies, upholding the divine side of the covenant. The image of God carrying the people is similar to the words of Isaiah 40:11. Verse 10 portrays the people's true response (disobedience), in contrast to what was expected of them.

Verses 11-14 describe the calling of Moses and the Exodus from Egypt. The prophet makes it clear that these miraculous events occurred by the hand of God.

The Prophet's Request (63:15–64:12)

Now the prophet asks God to intercede on behalf of the people. He begins by asking God to *look down from heaven and see* what is happening on earth. God is called *Father*, and this designation is contrasted to the meaning of *father* when it is attached to the patriarchs. God is father in the sense that God is present with the people and knows what is happening to them. Since the patriarchs were fathers in a more literal sense, they are no longer present to see what is going on.

Verses 17-19 form the heart of the lament. God has made the people disobedient by turning away from them. Therefore, says the prophet, if God would *return for the sake of thy servants* they would repent and return to God.

The whole of Chapter 64 is a prayer to God to relent and have compassion on the people. If God would return to the people, the earth would tremble (a traditional characteristic of God's appearance on earth).

Beginning at verse 5 (*Behold, thou wast angry*), the prophet speaks on behalf of the people, confessing their sin. They have become unclean; they no longer call upon the name of God. Then the prophet asks not that the sins be taken away, but that God's anger might abate (verse 9). After all, the people are now without a temple, and their land has become desolate. "How long must we suffer?" the prophet asks.

The People Rebelled (65:1-7)

Here God's answer to the prayer begins. The answer has three parts: (1) Yes, the people have rebelled against God (verses 1-7); (2) however, the people are God's servants (verses 8-16); and (3) God will bring about a change in the people's circumstances (verses 17-25). God speaks in the first person throughout this chapter.

In verses 1-2, God laments that the people did not respond properly in the past—God was *ready to be sought*, but the people ignored the invitation. Verse 2 portrays God, with hands outstretched, waiting for people who do not respond.

Verses 3-5 list other sins on the part of the people, all of which involve cultic worship. *Sacrificing in gardens* is a practice of the local Canaanite nature cults. The burning of incense is also a frequent part of cultic worship. *Sitting in tombs* refers to the practice of consulting the dead to receive oracles. Eating the flesh of swine was against Israelite law (see Deuteronomy 14:8).

The punishment is announced in verses 6-7. Curiously,

the address switches from second person (you) to third person (they). However, some Hebrew versions read *your* instead of *their*.

God's Servants (65:8-16)

Judgment is divided into two parts in these verses. God's *servants* are separated from the rest of the people and are promised salvation. According to verse 8, just as there are good and bad clusters of grapes, there are good and bad people. God promises not to *destroy them all*.

Sharon (verse 10) is a valley along the Mediterranean seacoast, in the northwestern part of the country. The Valley of Achor is at the northwestern end of the Dead Sea, near Jericho. Possession of these two areas means possession of the breadth of the land.

Set a table for Fortune and *fill cups of mixed wine for Destiny* (verse 11) refer to worship of Syrian gods Gad (which means *fortune*) and Meni (which means *destiny*).

Verses 13-16 describe the fate of the people. Whereas one group, the servants, will eat, drink, and rejoice, the rest of the people will be in anguish.

New Heavens and a New Earth (65:17-25)

God promises to create *new heavens and a new earth*. A similar circumstance is alluded to at the end of the Book of Revelation (see 21:1-4) and in Isaiah 66:22. The verb *create* is used often in Second Isaiah (see 42:5; 43:15; 48:7), and is the verb used when God creates heaven and earth in Genesis 1. This prophecy speaks about a new creation, of a restored Jerusalem.

The inhabitants of this new city will rejoice because they have been blessed by God. Women will not *bear children for calamity* (or sudden terror). In other words, the birth of children will take place naturally and in its time. In a similar way, work will not be done in vain. Labor will be rewarded.

Peace will reign in this restored city, symbolized by the

wolf and lamb living together in harmony. A similar image is portrayed in Isaiah 11:6-9.

Worship in the Temple (66:1-6)

In verses 1-2, God makes the point that the Temple, although it is the proper place for worship, is not the abode of God. Heaven is God's throne; the earth is God's footstool. Verses 3-4 continue the idea of worship, outlining what ritual practices are not acceptable and those that are acceptable. The first half of each line states an acceptable practice (*he who presents a cereal offering*), while the second half indicates what is not acceptable (*him who offers swine's blood*).

Verses 5 and 6 picture God's return to the city and the Temple, and punishment of Israel's enemies. *Those who tremble at his word* are those who practice true worship of God.

Jerusalem Will Rejoice (66:7-16)

Verses 7-9 describe the rebirth of the new Jerusalem. The bringing of the exiles back to Jerusalem is seen as a miracle performed by none other than God. Verses 10-14 portray the restored Jerusalem as a mother who will nurture her children and provide for them so that they might live abundantly. Jerusalem, formerly barren, will now have plenty of offspring. A similar image is described in Isaiah 49.

Verses 15-16 describe the coming of God, accompanied by wind and fire. These elements are common in Old Testament descriptions of God's epiphany. (See Isaiah 29:6, for example.)

The Glory of God (66:17-24)

According to verse 17, *in the midst* of the great procession will be persons who eat the flesh of swine and perform other similar abominations. According to God, these persons will all have a similar fate.

Verses 18-21 describe God's gathering of *all nations and tongues* into the restored city, in order to witness the glory of God. *Tarshish* is a city on the coast of Spain; *Put* and *Lud* are territories in Africa; *Javan* is on the coast of Asia Minor. Taken together, these peoples symbolize all nations everywhere. All these people will come in throngs to the new Jerusalem. Some of them will even become priests.

Verses 22-24 conclude the words of this prophet by drawing a sharp contrast. Those who will worship God will live forever through their descendants. Those who have rebelled, however, will live in eternal torment.

§ § § § § § §

The Message of Isaiah 63–66

These concluding chapters of the Book of Isaiah draw together many of the themes that are found throughout the book as a whole.

§ God has the capability and the willingness to punish the people if they disobey.

§ God's steadfast love is available to those who would become God's people.

§ When the people suffer, God suffers.

§ God's actions on behalf of the people in the past show God's intentions to protect the chosen people now and in the future.

§ Some cultic ritual is abhorrent to God.

§ God will distinguish between the righteous, deserving salvation, and the evil, deserving punishment.

§ The transformation of heaven and earth is the ultimate intention of God.

§ § § § § § §

Glossary of Terms

Acacia: A tree that grows in Israel, and the wood it produces. Acacia was used to build the ark of the covenant.

Achor, Valley of: A valley in the northern part of Judah. The name means *valley of trouble.*

Adrammelech: A son of Sennacherib, king of Assyria. He murdered his father in the temple of Nisroch.

Ahaz: King of Judah during part of the ministry of Isaiah. The son of Jotham. He reigned from 735–715 B.C.

Amorites: Those who lived in the region of Amurru, probably taking in Syria and part of Israel. Sometimes refers to the pre-Israelite population of Canaan.

Amulet: Jewelry that was believed to have magical powers. It was usually worn around the neck to ward off evil.

Ar: A Moabite city, possibly the capital of that region. Located on the Arnon River.

Ariel: Another name for Jerusalem. The word means *lion of God* or *hearth of God.*

Arpad: A city in northern Syria. It was destroyed by Assyria in the eighth century B.C.

Ashdod: One of five main Philistine cities on the coast.

Asherim: A goddess of the early Semitic religion, and the objects that were used to represent her in cultic worship.

Assyria: A Mesopotamian civilization that rose to power during the time of Isaiah's ministry (eighth century B.C.).

Babylon: The capital city of Babylonia, a Mesopotamian civilization in the area in between the Tigris and Euphrates.

Bath: A unit of liquid measure equal to the amount of an ephah (a dry measure); about five and a half gallons.

Beer-elim: A city in Moab; the name means *well of chiefs.*

Bel: The god of Babylon, symbol of the evil of that nation.

Bozrah: An important city in the territory of Edom, which was used by the prophets to symbolize the strength of that nation.

Brook of Egypt: A river flowing across the southern border of Canaan. It is referred to in records of Sargon and Sennacherib.
Brook of the Willows: A river in the region of Moab. The Moabites carried their belongings across this river in flight.
Burnt offering: Sacrifices burned on the altar in the Temple.
Calno: A city in Babylon, associated with Carchemish. It was probably located in the northern part of the country.
Carchemish: A city on the Euphrates River that was captured by the Assyrians during the time of Isaiah.
Chaldea: A territory in the southern portion of Babylonia. *Chaldean* is sometimes used synonymously with *Babylonian*.
Cyprus: An island in the Mediterranean Sea, northwest of Palestine's coast.
Cyrus: The Persian king who liberated Judah from the dominaton of Assyria in the sixth century B.C.
Damascus: The capital of Syria in biblical times. Allied with Israel against Judah in the Syro-Ephraimitic War (734 B.C.).
Dedanites: People living in the northwest portion of Arabia.
Dibon: A Moabite city mentioned by Isaiah in his oracles against Moab. The Moabite Stone was found there in 1868.
Dumah: Used in Isaiah 21:11, this word may be a variation of the name *Edom*. The word may also mean *silence*.
Elam: A territory in the Tigris valley; its capital was Susa.
Eliakim: The son of Hilkiah; servant in the court of Hezekiah.
Ephah: The name of an Arabian tribe. The word also means a dry measure equal to about half a bushel.
Ephraim: Ancestor of one of Israel's tribes; younger son of Joseph. Also refers to the territory that tribe occupied, in the central hill country.
Esarhaddon: Son of Sennacherib, king of Assyria in 681–669 B.C.
Hamath: A city on the Orontes River in Syria, conquered by the Assyrians.
Haran: A Mesopotamian city conquered by the Assyrians during the time of Isaiah.
Heshbon: A Moabite city located east of Jerusalem.
Hivites: People in Canaan before the arrival of the Israelites.
Homer: A unit of dry measure equaling five bushels.
Jahaz: City in the Transjordan, conquered by the Moabites.

Javan: A territory in the vicinity of Greece; inhabited by the descendants of Java, son of Japheth.

Joah: An official in the court of Hezekiah, sent by Hezekiah to the Assyrians.

Jotham: King of Judah during the time of Isaiah's ministry, from 742–735 B.C. He was the son of Uzziah.

Kedar: A son of Ishmael and the father of an Arabian tribe that lived in the desert.

Kir: A city in Moab; probably the same location as Kir-hareseth and Kir-heres.

Lachish: A city in Judah, located south of Jerusalem.

Leviathan: A mythical dragon in ancient creation stories.

Levites: Descendants of the tribe of Levi; responsible for cultic worship in the Temple.

Medes: Inhabitants of Media, a Mosopotamian territory.

Midian: A territory in northwest Arabia.

Moab: A country east of Palestine, across the Jordan.

Negeb: A desert-like area to the south of Palestine.

Nineveh: The capital of Assyria, located on the Tigris River.

Pekah: A king of Israel from 737–732 B.C.

Perazim, Mount: A mountain near the Valley of Rephaim.

Philistines: People living on the Mediterranean coast.

Rabshakeh: Cupbearer to the kings of Assyria and Babylon.

Rahab: A mythical dragon in ancient creation stories.

Rezin: A king of Syria during Isaiah's time.

Samaria: The capital city of the Northern Kingdom (Israel).

Sargon II: King of Assyria from 722–705 B.C. Son of Tiglath-Pileser III. Responsible for the fall of the Northern Kingdom.

Seir: The main mountain range in Edom.

Sennacherib: King of Assyria from 705–681 B.C..

Sharon: A plain in Palestine, from Joppa to Mount Carmel.

Sidon: A Phoenician city on the Mediterranean seacoast.

Tirhakah: An Egyptian king who allied with Hezekiah against Sennacherib.

Tyre: A city on the upper Meditarranean seacoast, often associated with Sidon.

Uzziah: A king of Judah from 783–742 B.C..

Waistcloth: A leather garment worn around the loins.

Guide to Pronunciation

Achor: Ah-CORE
Adrammelech: AH-druh-MEH-leck
Ahaz: AY-haz
Amorites: AA-more-ites
Ariel: Air-ee-ELL
Arnon: ARE-non
Arpad: ARE-pod
Asaph: Ah-SAHF
Ashdod: ASH-dod
Asherim: Ash-uh-REEM
Assyria: Ah-SEER-ee-ah
Baladan: BAH-lah-don
Bashan: Bah-SHAHN
Bozrah: BOZ-rah
Carchemish: CAR-keh-mish
Carmel: Car-MELL
Chaldeans: Kal-DEE-ans
Dedanites: DEH-duh-nites
Dibon: dih-BONE
Elam: EE-lum
Esarhaddon: Eh-shar-HAD-dun
Gozan: GOH-zahn
Hamath: HAY-math
Haran: Hah-RAHN
Heshbon: HESH-bon
Hilkiah: Hil-KIGH-uh
Hivites: HIH-vites

156

Horonaim: Hore-oh-NAY-yim
Ivvah: EE-vah
Jahaz: JAH-hahz
Javan JAH-van
Jazer JAH-zer
Jeshurun: JEH-shoo-run
Kedar: KEY-dar
Lachish: Lah-KEESH
Manasseh: Muh-NAS-seh
Medeba: Meh-deh-BAH
Molech: MOH-leck
Nebaioth: Neh-bah-YOTHE
Nisroch: NIZ-rock
Ophir: OH-fear
Pekah: PEH-kah
Perizim: Pare-eh-ZEEM
Rabshakeh: RAHB-sheh-keh
Rephaim: Reh-fah-EEM
Rezeph: REH-zeff
Rezin: REH-zin
Seir: Seh-EER
Sennacherib: Seh-NAA-keh-rib
Sharezer: Sheh-REE-zer
Shear-jashub: Sheh-ARE-yah-SHOOB
Sheol: Sheh-OLE
Sidon: SIGH-dun
Tabeel: Tah-buh-ELL
Tema: TAY-mah
Tirhakah: Tear-hah-KAH
Uzziah: You-ZIGH-ah
Zebulun: ZEB-you-lun
Zoan: ZOH-an
Zoar: ZOH-ar

Black
R. Sangarius
PHRYGIA
Gordion
Gomer
(Gimarrai)
Meshech
(Mushki)
R. Halys
Usiana
GREECE
Corinth
Athens
LYDIA
R. Hermus
Sardis
(Sepharad)
R. Maeander
JAVAN
CILICIA
(KHILAKKU)
Kue
Ura
Pitusu
Lycia
Rhodes
Crete
(Caphtor)
Cyprus
(Iadanna)
The Great Sea
(The Upper Sea, the Western Sea)
Arvad
Gebal (Byblos)
Berytus
Sidon
Tyre
Ushu
Acco
Megiddo
ISRAEL
Samaria
Jerusalem
JUDAH
Gaza
Raphia
Migdol
Pelusium
Libya
Sais
Zoan
(Tanis)
Tahpanhes
Athribis
Heliopolis
(On)
Memphis
(Noph)
EDOM
Sela
Sinai
EGYPT
R. Nile
Hermopolis
Lycopolis
(Siut)
Red Sea
Thebes
ETHIOPIA
Syene

THE ANCIENT NEAR EAST
IN THE TIME OF
THE ASSYRIAN EMPIRE

Approximate extent of Assyrian domination
in the latter part of the 8th. Century
(Later, under Esarhaddon (681-669), Assyria conquered Egypt)

From the *Oxford Bible Atlas*, Third Edition

PALESTINE IN
OLD TESTAMENT
TIMES

THE

GREAT

SEA

Plain of Sharon

ISRAEL

Megiddo

Jezreel

Valley of Jezreel

Hazor

Sea of
Chinnereth

GESHUR

B A S H A N

Ramoth-G

Samaria   •Tirzah

Shechem

Hill Country
of
Ephraim

Shiloh

Joppa

Bethel

Gezer

Gibeon

Gibeah

Jerusalem

Ekron

Ashdod•

Ashkelon.

J U D A H

Gath

Gaza

Hebron Kiriath-arba

Jericho

Salt

Sea

(Sea of
the Arabah)

Heshbon

Beer-sheba

Kir-haresheth

From the *Oxford Bible Atlas*, Third Edit